S. HRG. 113–152

# REVERSING IRAN'S NUCLEAR PROGRAM

## HEARING

BEFORE THE

## COMMITTEE ON FOREIGN RELATIONS UNITED STATES SENATE

ONE HUNDRED THIRTEENTH CONGRESS

FIRST SESSION

OCTOBER 3, 2013

Printed for the use of the Committee on Foreign Relations

Available via the World Wide Web: http://www.gpo.gov/fdsys/

U.S. GOVERNMENT PRINTING OFFICE

86–351 PDF     WASHINGTON : 2014

For sale by the Superintendent of Documents, U.S. Government Printing Office
Internet: bookstore.gpo.gov   Phone: toll free (866) 512–1800; DC area (202) 512–1800
Fax: (202) 512–2104   Mail: Stop IDCC, Washington, DC 20402 0001

## COMMITTEE ON FOREIGN RELATIONS

ROBERT MENENDEZ, New Jersey, *Chairman*

BARBARA BOXER, California
BENJAMIN L. CARDIN, Maryland
JEANNE SHAHEEN, New Hampshire
CHRISTOPHER A. COONS, Delaware
RICHARD J. DURBIN, Illinois
TOM UDALL, New Mexico
CHRISTOPHER MURPHY, Connecticut
TIM KAINE, Virginia
EDWARD J. MARKEY, Massachusetts

BOB CORKER, Tennessee
JAMES E. RISCH, Idaho
MARCO RUBIO, Florida
RON JOHNSON, Wisconsin
JEFF FLAKE, Arizona
JOHN McCAIN, Arizona
JOHN BARRASSO, Wyoming
RAND PAUL, Kentucky

DANIEL E. O'BRIEN, *Staff Director*
LESTER E. MUNSON III, *Republican Staff Director*

(II)

# CONTENTS

# REVERSING IRAN'S NUCLEAR PROGRAM

---

### THURSDAY, OCTOBER 3, 2013

U.S. SENATE,
COMMITTEE ON FOREIGN RELATIONS,
*Washington, DC.*

The committee met, pursuant to notice, at 10 a.m., in room SD–419, Dirksen Senate Office Building, Hon. Robert Menendez (chairman of the committee) presiding.

Present: Senators Menendez, Cardin, Shaheen, Coons, Kaine, Markey, Corker, Risch, Rubio, Johnson, and McCain.

### OPENING STATEMENT OF HON. ROBERT MENENDEZ, U.S. SENATOR FROM NEW JERSEY

The CHAIRMAN. Good morning. This hearing of the Senate Foreign Relations Committee will come to order.

We are here today under unusual circumstances, but nevertheless ready to fulfill our constitutional duty to oversee national security policy, foreign policy, international economic policy as it relates to safeguarding America's interests abroad. That is our fundamental duty.

And we have convened today to ensure that the world understands that a shutdown of Government in the United States is not a shutdown of American interests and obligations abroad.

Having said that, we are pleased to have with us a familiar face to the committee, Under Secretary of State for Political Affairs Wendy Sherman. She is here to help shed light on U.S. policy toward Iran, given the change in leadership and recent statements of President Rouhani, and to provide her perspective on behalf of the Department on the way ahead on the nuclear issue.

On our second panel today, we have three distinguished experts from the private sector: Dr. David Albright, a physicist who is the founder and president of the Institute for Science and International Security and who has written extensively on secret nuclear weapons programs around the world; Ambassador Jim Jeffrey, a distinguished visiting fellow at the Washington Institute, where he is focused on Iran's efforts to expand its influence in the region; and Dr. Ray Takeyh, a senior fellow at the Council on Foreign Relations and a former senior adviser on Iran at the State Department. We look forward to all of your testimonies and thoughts on the status and the future of United States-Iran policy.

Before we hear from our panelists, let me restate concerns that I have expressed publicly and will express again for the record. In my view, the sanctions have worked to bring us to this pivotal point, and the fundamental question is now whether the Iranians are ready to actually conclude an agreement with the international community; whether they are prepared to turn rhetoric into action.

In the lead-up to last week's U.N. General Assembly meeting, I was cautiously hopeful about what we would hear. But in my personal view, the new face of Iran looked and sounded very much like the old face, with a softer tone and a smoother edge. Although Iran's messenger may have changed in the last election, the message seems to have remained the same.

The questions are these: Should we be cautiously hopeful for a diplomatic solution, given the new leadership and rhetoric coming from Tehran? What are the administration's near-term diplomatic goals and objectives for the P5+1 negotiations? How do we test Iranian intentions that they are negotiating in good faith? How do we get Iran to commit to transparency and to allow full verification that it has abandoned its pursuit of a nuclear weapons capability?

Until we have the answers to these questions, it is my view that we must sustain the pressure on Iran and maintain the credible military threat that has brought Iran to the table.

Now it is clear that while we are talking about Iran, its centrifuges are still spinning. In the last 2 years, it has installed thousands of additional centrifuges, and although it is not enriching in all of them, the vast majority are fully installed and under vacuum, meaning Iran could quickly double its enrichment capacity.

The fact is these expanded capabilities are reducing the time Iran needs to quickly produce a sufficient amount of weapons-grade uranium. The fear is that Iran will achieve a breakout capability, defined as the technical capability to produce sufficient weapon-grade uranium for a nuclear device without being detected by the international community.

According to the work of one of our panelists, David Albright of the Institute for Science and International Security, if Iran continues to expand its centrifuges at its current pace, it will be able to produce by mid-2014 enough material for one bomb within a period of several weeks. It is an open question as to whether the international community would be able to detect a breakout if it would occur this quickly.

Iran is also nearing completion of a heavy water reactor in Iraq. If that reactor operates, Iran could create a plutonium pathway to nuclear weapons, enough plutonium each year for one or two nuclear weapons.

From my perspective, as long as Iran is actively pursuing its nuclear program, we must actively work to increase the pressure. This is no less than what is required by multiple U.N. Security Council resolutions. And while we welcome Iran's diplomatic overtures, they cannot be used to buy time, avoid sanctions, and continue the march toward a nuclear weapons capability.

I welcome President Rouhani's announcement at the U.N. General Assembly, and the Supreme Leader's fatwa that Iran seeks a peaceful resolution to international concerns about Iran's nuclear program and is committed to a peaceful nuclear program. But compliance with the U.N. Security Council resolutions, in my view, would be the ultimate test of Iran's intentions.

Let me conclude by restating my belief that the sanctions regime in place thus far has been critical in compelling the Iranian

Government back to the negotiating table. If the sanctions were not hurting, we would not have heard so much about them in President Rouhani's speech. What is important now is what Iran does, not what it says. We do not need more words. What we would like to see is its compliance with the four U.N. Security Council resolutions and the suspension of uranium enrichment.

Some of us are moving forward with a new round of sanctions that will require further reduction in purchases of Iranian petroleum. But we are also serious about relief from sanctions if the Iranian Government meets its Security Council responsibilities.

With that, let me turn to Senator Corker for his opening statement.

## OPENING STATEMENT OF HON. BOB CORKER, U.S. SENATOR FROM TENNESSEE

Senator CORKER. Well, thank you, Mr. Chairman.

I know there was some discussion about whether having a hearing today or not having a hearing today in light of the circumstances was the right thing to do. But I do appreciate very much your focus on Iran and some of the threats that our Nation faces.

And I want to say that we have had, since you have been chairman, a number of really important issues to deal with, and I know that this is going to be one of the most important that we deal with over the next several months. And I do appreciate the diligence that is being put forth. I also want to thank you for the efforts that you and Mark Kirk, together, have put forth relative to sanctions.

And just as in the Syrian debate, you know, where we had people with differing viewpoints, all of which I thought were very respectful and thoughtful, I really was proud—regardless of where people came out, I was really proud of the way the committee handled itself with humility and soberness.

And so, as we deal with this issue, I want to start by saying still the greatest threat to our Nation, the greatest threat still is ourselves. And it is our inability to deal with our fiscal matters in an appropriate way. And I think today's meeting in light of a Government shutdown still points to that.

This, on the other hand, is a grave threat to world peace. And again, I thank you for the way that we are going about this, and I hope that what we will do together as a committee after testimony from these two panels—and I know some potential activities that will take place in the Banking Committee—is that we will be prudent about how we go forth with these.

I do believe the sanctions that we have put in place have created this moment, and I do know that the administration, in fairness, opposed some of those sanctions. And we had to sort of push the administration to the table, and yet I will say the administration now is trying to take advantage of those.

So I hope that together, through intelligent testimony and thoughtfulness, I hope we will move ahead in a fashion that shows a real strategy, that causes Congress to help push these negotiations along and push to ensure that what Iran does is real. It is not just talk.

So I thank you very much for the sentiments. I thank you for your previous efforts. I look forward to the testimony today, and I look forward to this committee and the Banking Committee acting in unison in a way that produces a result here, which is what all of us want to see.

So thank you very much.

The CHAIRMAN. Thank you, Senator Corker, and we appreciate your work and your leadership as well with us.

With that, we will recognize Secretary Sherman. Your full statement will be included in the record, without objection, and the floor is yours.

## STATEMENT OF HON. WENDY SHERMAN, UNDER SECRETARY FOR POLITICAL AFFAIRS, U.S. DEPARTMENT OF STATE, WASHINGTON, DC

Ambassador SHERMAN. Thank you very much.

Chairman Menendez, Ranking Member Corker, distinguished members of the committee, thank you for inviting me to be here today, even during these difficult times. It is always welcome to return to the Senate and speak with you about an issue we both agree—we all agree—is one of our country's primary foreign policy and national security challenges.

Today, I plan to speak about recent talks with the Iranian Government at the U.N. General Assembly in New York of which I was a part, the status of our negotiations, our continued effort to put pressure on the Iranian Government, and a potential path forward for diplomacy, including the core actions needed to reach a verifiable agreement with Iran.

Let me start with a very brief survey of our dual-track policy to show how we arrived at this point. As President Obama has said many times, the United States remains committed to preventing Iran from obtaining a nuclear weapon. The strategy we have pursued—and continue to pursue—to fulfill this commitment is the dual-track policy of engagement and pressure.

While our preference has always been diplomatic engagement, we concluded that such engagement would not work absent meaningful pressure. In response, we and our allies, with the President's and your very crucial leadership, established one of the toughest sanctions regimes the world has ever seen. As a result, 23 economies have united in significantly reducing or eliminating purchases of Iranian crude oil.

Over the past 24 months, Iran's rial has depreciated by approximately 60 percent, as Iran's access to the international financial sector has been largely severed. Indeed, in the runup to his election this June, President Rouhani made the case that the failure to pursue a serious agreement on the nuclear file and the international sanctions that resulted from that failure was devastating the Iranian economy.

I would emphasize that it was the Iranian Government's choices that led to these devastating sanctions, and it will be the Iranian Government's actions in the months ahead that will be a key factor in determining whether we decide the sanctions should remain in place or whether we can begin to relieve some sanction pressure as Iran addresses our concern.

President Rouhani says he has a mandate—both a popular mandate from the Iranian people and a mandate from Supreme Leader

Khamenei—to pursue an agreement that satisfies the international community's concerns over Iran's nuclear program. As the President reaffirmed last week, we are prepared to test that proposition in a serious way. In doing so, we must remain mindful of the long history of Iranian deception regarding its nuclear program and insist that Iran's new tone be met as soon as possible by new and concrete and verifiable actions.

We must also do our part to ensure the success of this effort and to avoid any measures that could prematurely inhibit our ability to secure a diplomatic solution. The process for testing Iran's intentions began last week in New York. There, on the margins of the U.N. General Assembly, Secretary Kerry and I met Foreign Minister Zarif and the Foreign Ministers of the P5+1.

In that meeting, as in all of our exchanges with the Iranian Government, including the Secretary's bilateral with Foreign Minister Zarif, we made clear that we seek an agreement that respects the right of the Iranian people to access peaceful nuclear energy while ensuring to the world that Iran meets its responsibilities under the Nuclear Nonproliferation Treaty and U.N. Security Council resolutions.

Foreign Minister Zarif gave a thoughtful presentation. He told us that Iran does not seek nuclear weapons and detailed the reasons why it did not make sense for Iran to possess nuclear weapons.

We also made clear in return that his words alone, while welcome, are not enough. So in the coming weeks, we will look to the Iranian Government to translate its words into transparent, meaningful, and verifiable actions. We enter this period with our eyes wide open. As Secretary Kerry has said, no deal is better than a bad deal.

Now it is time to see if negotiations can begin in earnest. Let me give you an idea of how we see this moving forward.

Given the scope of Iran's nuclear program and its history of noncompliance with U.N. Security Council resolutions, as well as the deep mistrust between our two countries, any productive path forward must include confidence-building through meaningful, transparent, and verifiable steps. We will be looking for specific steps by Iran that address core issues including, but not limited to, the pace and scope of its enrichment program, the transparency of its overall nuclear program, and stockpiles of enriched uranium.

The Iranians, in return, will doubtless be seeking some relief from the comprehensive international sanctions that are now in place. We have been clear that only concrete, viable steps, and verifiable steps can offer a path to sanctions relief. We look forward to hearing Foreign Minister Zarif's suggested plan, which he says he will bring to us when the P5+1 meet next with the Iranian delegation in Geneva on October 15 and 16.

Let me assure you that we will continue to vigorously enforce the sanctions that are in place as we explore a negotiated resolution and will be especially focused on sanctions evasion and efforts by Iranians to relieve the pressure.

I must note here, if I may, Mr. Chairman, to take an extra moment and note, however, our ability to do that—to enforce sanctions, to stop sanctions invaders—is being hampered significantly by the shutdown. I think many of you will have seen an article by Josh Rogan and Eli Lake today that ''Government Shutdown Empties Offices Enforcing Sanctions on Iran.''

OFAC, which is in the Treasury Department, which really oversees much of this, along with our own sanctions monitoring group, has been completely, virtually utterly depleted in this time. In addition, the intelligence community, which we rely on for intelligence information to go after sanctions evaders and sanctions people who are not paying attention to the sanctions, as the DNI said, General Clapper, the other day, has been devastated as well—more than 60 percent reduced during the shutdown.

So we will do our best to enforce these sanctions, to stop sanctions invaders, but I sincerely hope that the shutdown ends soon so that we are truly able to do so in the runup and as these negotiations proceed.

As we move forward, it will be critical that we continue to move together and take no steps that signal divisions to Iran that it could and likely would exploit. Further, as the effect of our sanctions on Iran depends in part on the actions of our partners, we must ensure that our sanctions do not place an undue burden on those countries. It is not in our interest to create fissures within the international coalition facing Iran, as the impact of our pressure comes from the steps these countries take.

We will also continue to raise our other concerns, including Iran's sponsorship of terrorist organizations, human rights abuses, and destabilizing activities across the region. And we will remain absolutely dedicated to the return of U.S. citizen, Robert Levinson, and United States-Iranian dual nationals, Saeed Abedini and Amir Hekmati.

Indeed, both the President and the Secretary of State raised these cases with the Iranians. Every day their families wait for them to come home.

So, as we do, we will remain in close consultations with our allies and partners in the region, including Israel, whose security remains a paramount focus. We will also continue our close consultation with you and with other Members of the Congress, as we have in the past, so that any congressional action is aligned with our negotiating strategy as we move forward.

Thank you again for this opportunity to discuss with this committee the important developments over the past week in New York. As always, I look forward to regular engagement with you in the weeks ahead and to your questions and comments today.

Thank you.

[The prepared statement of Ambassador Sherman follows:]

PREPARED STATEMENT OF UNDER SECRETARY OF STATE WENDY R. SHERMAN

INTRODUCTION

Chairman Menendez, Ranking Member Corker, distinguished members of the committee, thank you for inviting me to be here today. It is always a pleasure to return to the Senate and speak with you about an issue we both agree is one of our country's primary foreign policy challenges.

This hearing comes at a pivotal time for U.S. policy toward Iran. As requested, I will speak about recent talks with the Iranian Government at the U.N. General Assembly in New York, the status of our negotiations, our continued effort to put pressure on the Iranian Government, and a potential path forward for diplomacy—including the core actions needed to reach a verifiable agreement with Iran.

## DUAL TRACK POLICY AND ROUHANI'S ELECTION

Let me start with a brief survey of our dual track policy to show how we arrived at this point.

As President Obama has stated many times, the United States remains committed to preventing Iran from obtaining a nuclear weapon.

The strategy we have pursued—and continue to pursue—to fulfill this commitment and address the international community's concerns with Iran's nuclear program is the dual track policy of engagement and pressure. While our preference has always been diplomatic engagement, we concluded that such engagement would not work absent pressure.

In response, we and our allies, with the President's and your leadership, have established a robust sanctions regime. I would emphasize that it was the Iranian Government's choices that led to these devastating sanctions, and it will be the Iranian Government's actions in the months ahead that will be a key factor in determining whether we decide the sanctions should remain in place or whether we can begin to relieve some sanctions pressure as Iran addresses our concerns.

The pressure on Iran has been severe and may lay the groundwork for a diplomatic outcome that addresses our concerns. However, we remain clear-eyed about the challenges ahead and the importance of vigilance, while proceeding in good faith. Through our continued efforts and the work of the Congress—notably through the leadership of the chairman of this committee, with the support of the ranking member—we have leveraged our economic influence effectively to raise the financial stakes for the Iranian Government.

In aggregate, we have led the international community in implementing an unprecedented sanctions regime that is having a real and tangible impact. Twenty-three economies have united in significantly reducing or eliminating purchases of Iranian crude oil. In 18 months, Iranian oil exports were cut by more than 1 million barrels per day. Iran's rial has depreciated by approximately 60 percent over the past 24 months. GDP has contracted by over 5 percent in the same period. Iran's access to the international financial sector has been largely severed and its ability to engage in normal economic activity has been sharply curtailed.

The Iranian Presidential election last June focused on the economy. Questions of how to engage with the international community on the nuclear file were front and center as President Rouhani, a former nuclear negotiator himself, ran against candidates that included then-current negotiator Saeed Jalili. Rouhani made the case that the failure to pursue a serious agreement on Iran's nuclear program was devastating the Iranian economy—and he won the election.

President Rouhani says he has a mandate—both a popular mandate from the Iranian people and a mandate from Supreme Leader Khamenei—to secure sanctions relief and improve Iran's economic situation, which can only be accomplished by pursuing an agreement that satisfies the international community's concerns over Iran's nuclear program.

As the President reaffirmed last week, we are prepared to test that proposition in a serious way. But we must do our part to ensure the success of this effort and to avoid any measures that could prematurely inhibit our ability to secure a diplomatic solution. Here it will be important that we—the Executive and U.S. Congress—remain in close consultation with each other, and that we ensure we can continue to show the Iranian Government that the international community remains firmly united as we begin this process.

## REVIEW OF LAST WEEK'S P5+1 MEETING

Last week, Secretary Kerry and I met with Foreign Minister Zarif and the Foreign Ministers of the P5+1 countries in New York on the margins of the U.N. General Assembly. Although we have indicated we are open to bilateral dialogue with the Iranians, we have emphasized that a nuclear deal would be concluded and implemented by the P5+1.

In our New York meeting, we made clear that we seek an agreement that respects the right of the Iranian people to access peaceful nuclear energy while ensuring to the world that Iran meets its responsibilities under the Nuclear Non-Proliferation Treaty and U.N. Security Council resolutions.

Foreign Minister Zarif gave a thoughtful presentation and set forth some ideas on how to proceed. He told us that Iran does not seek nuclear weapons and detailed the reasons why it did not make sense for Iran to possess nuclear weapons. We also made clear in return that his words alone, while welcome, are not enough. The test will lie in Iran's actions, to include the development and implementation of specific confidence-building measures as well as actions that ultimately address all of our concerns.

So in the coming weeks, we will be looking to the Iranian Government to translate its words into transparent, meaningful, and verifiable actions. We enter this period hopeful, but sober. As Secretary Kerry said, no deal is better than a bad deal. So now it is time to see if negotiations can begin in earnest and generate a positive result.

### FUTURE PROSPECTS

Let me give you an idea of how we see this process moving forward.

Given the scope of Iran's nuclear program and its history of noncompliance with IAEA Board of Governors and U.N. Security Council resolutions, as well as the deep mistrust between our two countries, any productive path forward must start with mutual confidence building.

Meaningful, transparent, and verifiable steps are necessary. We will be looking for specific steps by Iran that address core issues; including but not limited to the pace and scope of its enrichment program, the transparency of its overall nuclear program, and stockpiles of enriched uranium. The Iranians, in turn, will doubtless be seeking some relief from the comprehensive international sanctions that are now in place. We have been clear that only concrete verifiable steps can offer a path to sanctions relief. We look forward to hearing Foreign Minister Zarifs suggested plan when the P5+1 next meet with the Iranian delegation in Geneva on October 15 and 16.

We need to ensure throughout that the international community remains united and does not permit sanctions to prematurely unravel. Let me assure you that we will also continue to vigorously enforce the sanctions that are in place as we explore a negotiated resolution, and will be especially focused on sanctions evasion and efforts by the Iranians to relieve the pressure.

### CONCLUDING THOUGHTS

We are mindful of the serious challenges ahead. But we are also prepared to move expeditiously in pursuit of a diplomatic resolution to this crisis. If there is indeed a diplomatic outcome available, then it is one we must test with good faith and due diligence.

As the President said after his phone call with President Rouhani, "the very fact that this [phone call] was the first communication between an American and Iranian President since 1979 underscores the deep mistrust between our countries, but it also indicates the prospect of moving beyond that difficult history."

Any path to a meaningful agreement will be difficult. Both sides have significant concerns that will have to be overcome. Both sides will also have to demonstrate to one another's satisfaction that any understanding that is reached will be fully implemented. We are prepared to pursue this diplomatic track along with our P5+1 partners, and hope that Iran's actions soon live up to their words.

As we move forward, it will be critical that we continue to move together and take no steps that signal divisions to Iran that it could and likely would exploit. Further, as the effect of our sanctions on Iran depends in part on the actions of our partners, we must ensure that our sanctions do not place an undue burden on those countries. It is not in our interest to create fissures within the international coalition facing Iran, as the impact of our pressure comes from the steps these countries take.

We will continue to raise our other concerns, including Iran's sponsorship of terrorist organizations, human rights abuses, and destabilizing activities across the region. And we will remain dedicated to the return of U.S. citizen Robert Levinson and U.S.-Iranian dual nationals Saeed Abedini and Amir Hekmati. Every day their families wait for them to come home.

And as we do, we will remain in close consultations with our allies and partners in the region, including Israel, whose security remains a paramount focus. We also hope to continue our close consultation with the Congress, as we have in the past, so that any congressional action is aligned with our negotiating strategy as we move forward.

Thank you again for this opportunity to discuss with this committee the important developments over the past week in New York. As always, I look forward to regular engagement with you in the weeks ahead and to your questions and comments today.

The CHAIRMAN. Thank you, Madam Secretary.

Let me start off, and there is so much here. But I heard a sentence in your statement, and I get a little concerned. And let me make it very clear from my perspective that when we start talking about relieving sanctions as the Iranians begin to alleviate our concerns, you know, I am not sure exactly what we mean by "begin to alleviate our concerns."

You know, there is a real, legitimate concern here that the Iranians will do a certain amount that ultimately begins to create some sanction relief. But at the end of the day, that draws back the international community, that draws back the forces of keeping the pressure that has brought us to this moment. And then to gear that back up would be an incredibly difficult proposition.

So I listen to the words, but Iran has repeatedly said that they reject the development and use of nuclear weapons. And that has been reiterated now. But how believable is that statement, given what we know about Iran's history that prior assessments that have been brought before this committee, both I think in public as well as in private, that Iran has previously, at the government's direction, sought a nuclear weapons program?

So they still, as far as I know, have not admitted that they were pursuing a nuclear weapons program. They still say they reject that, unless that has happened at the P5+1 negotiations and we have not heard about it. What are we talking about here in terms of relieving sanctions if they begin to alleviate our concerns? And how do we reconcile what the Iranians are saying now with what is a verified history of moving toward a nuclear weapons program?

So I get concerned about that. And the final element of this, so that I can package it so you can give me a response, is President Rouhani has been very clear and proud of the fact, as is evidenced by his book, that last time he conducted negotiations over Iran's nuclear program, he was able to use those negotiations as a stalling tactic while his government advanced its nuclear program.

I look at all of those realities, and I get concerned. I understand the need to test the diplomatic possibility. But by the same token, I get concerned when I hear about easing of sanctions to satisfy some of our concerns.

Ambassador SHERMAN. Mr. Chairman, I think this is a very legitimate concern and one that we have thought through very carefully as we move ahead to these negotiations. We quite agree with you.

The fundamental large sanctions that we have in place should not disappear any time soon unless all of our concerns are addressed by the Iranians. And with that, we agree with you because we do not want the sanctions regime to fall apart.

At the same time, the reason we also focus on confidence-building, some early test, whether that is some degradation of their current posture, some freeze, some pause—there are many ways to do this—is because every day their nuclear program goes forward. And to get to a comprehensive agreement will take some time because there are highly technical issues here that take some time to negotiate. It is not like you can do this over a 48-hour period. It will take more time than that to do so.

So since we know they are continuing with their nuclear program and because of the history that you point out when Rouhani was the chief negotiator 2003 to 2005, we know that deception is part of the DNA. We want to make sure that we can put some time on the clock for those comprehensive negotiations.

So what we are thinking through is what is it that would give us some confidence today, would put some time on the clock, stop their nuclear program from moving forward while we get to that comprehensive agreement that it would allow the full   sanctions relief they are looking for? There may be some elements that we can do initially if they take verifiable, concrete action that will put time on the clock that are reversible or, in fact, do not go to any of the key sanctions that have brought them to the table. So this is the issue.

The CHAIRMAN. Let us talk about the time on the clock.

Ambassador SHERMAN. Sure.

The CHAIRMAN. David Albright, who will follow you on the second panel, provides some very detailed information about the status of Iran's nuclear program that is very concerning, indicating that Iran will soon have the ability to break out in a time period as short as 2 weeks to several months. Is that an assessment you concur with?

Ambassador SHERMAN. What I would say is I can give you in this setting, and we would be glad to have a classified briefing with our intelligence community and give you our detailed assessment. I am not going to do that here publicly because, quite frankly, I would not want Iran to know what our assessment is about how much time there is.

The CHAIRMAN. So let us assume that Mr. Albright's assessment is right. I am not saying you will—for argument's sake, let us assume his assessment is right. If that assessment is right, then your timeframe for definitive action is relatively short.

Ambassador SHERMAN. We believe that we have some time, but we do not have a lot of time. I would agree with that statement.

I would also say that what we have said publicly is from the time that the Supreme Leader decides that he truly wants to go for a nuclear weapon—and we do not believe he has yet made that fundamental decision but wants to put the pieces in place that give him that option—it could take as much as a year before he got there. Now there are many factors here that change that clock, and I have tremendous regard for Dr. Albright, and so I would listen carefully to him for sure.

But I think it would probably be best for us to have that classified briefing with the committee and tell you all of the elements that change that clock. Let me give you one example.

Last year, the—not at this U.N. General Assembly, but a year ago—the Prime Minister of Israel put a very key element on the table, and that is how much quantity stockpile of enriched uranium Iran might have that they could then easily convert to 90 percent enriched uranium, which then would give them the material they needed for a nuclear weapon, if they had weaponization, if they had a delivery mechanism, all of which is in the future.

What the Iranians did, however, is they started to convert their enriched uranium into oxide. And even though it can be changed back, that takes some time. So the Iranians very smartly changed the calculus of the clock by converting that enriched uranium to oxide.

So calculating the time clock here is very complicated, which is why I would like to do it in a classified session. What I will say, though, is every single day, our intelligence community, at least when we have them full time, which we do not at the moment— but we are still focused on this, even with the staff we have—look at where the Iranians are on a variety of factors because all of those factors change the clock.

The CHAIRMAN. And I will just move on by saying part of the equation here is our ability to detect a nuclear breakout by Iran, and that is not with scientific precision here. And so, that is part of our challenge as to how close to the line do you let them go?

Senator Corker.

Senator CORKER. Thank you, Mr. Chairman.

And Secretary, thank you for your testimony and your job on behalf of our country.

I do not think there is any question but that the actions that this committee and others have taken, and Congress in general, toward Iran have helped put us in the place we are in. I know that the administration touted the fact that this committee passed an authorization for the use of military force as being one of those things that moved Syria into a place where they were willing to negotiate. And you know, we will see as history plays out whether that was, in fact, the case and what the outcome is going to be.

Obviously, there are a lot of questions about what is happening on the negotiating front. I guess what I would ask you relative to us is, what is it you would like for us to do in the interim to support the outcome? I know there have been discussions about additional sanctions. There have been discussions about things even more draconian than that at a date in the future if nothing changes.

What is it that you would like to see us do to support a successful conclusion here? Would you like for us to move ahead with additional sanctions?

Ambassador SHERMAN. Thank you, Senator.

First of all, I do want to thank this committee for the vote you took on Syria. I know it was very difficult, but I do believe it was helpful.

I was with the Secretary in the negotiations with Lavrov in Geneva for the agreement and very much part of all of the discussions on the U.N. Security Council resolution and OPCW and looking ahead to the Geneva Conference on Syria. And the action by this committee to say that there was a credible threat of force in Syria was absolutely critical to our ability to move forward on CW.

So I thank you, Mr. Chairman. I thank you, Ranking Member Mr. Corker, and all of the members of the committee, for the action that you took. I know it was quite difficult, but it was—I do want to tell you, having experienced it, it was quite meaningful.

Secondly, in terms of Iran, I think that your holding this hearing today is important. I actually told the Iranians on the margins of the P5+1 meeting that I would testify, and they would hear from me that we were glad for what the President, President Rouhani had said, what Foreign Minister Zarif had said. But that words would not be enough. That they had to come to Geneva with actions, that Zarif had to present a plan.

So I thank you for this opportunity because it is important for them to hear the messages you are delivering and the message I am delivering in public that Secretary Kerry said in Tokyo. Just today, you saw on the morning news where he said again a no deal is better than a bad deal, that we are doing this with our eyes open. So this public discussion is very important to the negotiation.

Secondly, on your encouraging us to enforce the sanctions, to get all the assets in place to do so is equally critical, and the oversight you provide in that regard very helpful. In terms of legislation that is currently being discussed here on the Hill, we do believe it would be helpful for you all to at least allow this meeting to happen on the 15th and 16th of October before moving forward to consider those new sanctions.

And the reason I say that is because I want to be able to say to Iran, this is your—and I am saying it here today because they will listen to all of this. This is your opportunity. Come on the 15th of October with concrete, substantive actions that you will take, commitments you will make in a verifiable way, monitoring and verification that you will sign up to, to create some faith that there is reality to this, and our Congress will listen.

But I can assure you if you do not come on the 15th and 16th with that substantive plan that is real and verifiable, our Congress will take action, and we will support them to do so. So I would hope that you will allow us the time to begin these negotiations and see if, in fact, there is anything real here. With my telling of the Iranians quite directly that if there is not, that everyone is ready to act.

Senator CORKER. Well, that is a pretty clear answer and one I did not really expect. We have been getting some mixed signals from others within the administration. So I think what you have just said is that if Iran does not come to the table in mid-October in the way that they should, that you would fully support this committee and the Banking Committee and the Congress in general adding additional tough sanctions on Iran?

Ambassador SHERMAN. We would very much look forward to working with you on figuring out what those sanctions ought to be and how to proceed forward. So I cannot commit today for the administration that I agree with every line in legislation that is currently pending. But we will certainly want to go back to looking at what pressure needs to be added; yes.

Senator CORKER. And in interim, to alleviate any concerns that any of us might have, we pass laws here, and it is up to the executive branch to implement those. And I think what I am hearing you say is that throughout these negotiations, the administration is absolutely going to continue to put pressure on and continue to process and do all those things necessary to keep the existing sanctions working in a better way each day.

Is that correct?

Ambassador SHERMAN. That is correct, Senator. We will continue to enforce them with one caveat, that the shutdown does make it more difficult for us to do so because we do not have OFAC. We do not have our full intelligence committee. The State Department is putting restrictions on travel by State Department employees, and we use our sanctions team to travel the world, to go after sanctions evaders and folks who are not following through.

So it will limit our ability to do that. So, quite frankly, where Iran is concerned, the sooner the shutdown is over, the better we will be able to do the job you are asking us to do and that we want to do.

Senator CORKER. So, Mr. Chairman, if I could just ask one more question? My time is up, and I appreciate very much your testimony today. I know that you do not want to talk about publicly where we think Iran's capabilities are. I think most of us have a pretty good idea based on the many classified meetings we have been involved in.

But it has been my sense that the appropriate length of time to give Iran and the United States to come to a conclusion is 2 to 3 months. So let us move away from what their capabilities are, just to give us a sense as far as how we might be most productive here, would you agree that that is an appropriate timeframe for us to allow negotiations to come to a fruitful conclusion?

Ambassador SHERMAN. Senator, to be perfectly frank about it, I think I will have a better answer to that question after the meeting in Geneva on the 15th and 16th. It really depends on how fast they are ready to go.

Now you heard various things from the Iranians in New York. We heard them say that they could complete an agreement, a comprehensive agreement, and implement that agreement within a year. That is what Zarif said to us.

I think they can get to agreement. When we said we wanted to go faster than that, he said we could get to an agreement faster than that, we could not implement it in that period of time. And it probably cannot be implemented in that period of time because— in 3 to 6 months because there are a lot of highly technical things that have to be put in place.

But I do think you are correct to say that we will know in the next short period of time whether there is anything serious and real here or not.

Senator CORKER. Mr. Chairman, thank you.

And Madam Secretary, thank you.

The CHAIRMAN. Senator Cardin.

Senator CARDIN. Thank you, Mr. Chairman.

And Secretary Sherman, thank you very much for your public service. Thank you for being here today and underscoring a point that this shutdown is really hurting this country in so many ways; so many ways.

The success of dealing with Iran, and I understand your two tracks of pressure and diplomacy, very much depends upon our ability to carry out what we say we are going to do. And we have to be able to monitor that. We have to be able to get the intelligence on that. We have to be able to understand what is happening around the world.

And any diminishment of that capacity could have a major impact here. So there is many reasons why we should resolve this issue today about the Government remaining open. Not tomorrow, today it should be done. And you are just giving us one additional reason, and I thank you for that.

I want to go, underscore the point that the chairman made. It is not just what we do, as far as sanctions against Iran and keeping the pressure going, it is what the international community does. It is the enforcements. And it is what the United States position is with the international community.

And I think we all agree that we would like to see diplomacy work. We would like to see Iran move in the right direction and be able to monitor and make sure it occurs. But when we use language such as we are prepared to look at the sanctions if Iran makes significant progress or does certain things, it seems to me the international community may interpret it differently than we do.

Just the fact that we are meeting today has put additional pressures on international capitals to look at reducing some of its pressure on Iran. Many of our closest allies could do more in reducing their oil consumptions from Iran. They could do more.

It seems to me that if we are to be successful in the pressure to get Iran to give you not just the offer we are looking for, but the actions that are needed, that we need to increase the pressure, not reduce the pressure on Iran at this point. And that, yes, it means what we do, but what we do in working with our coalition to say now is the time to reduce your oil purchases from Iran, not to increase it. And the world oil market right now is favorable for us to really reduce even more.

So I guess my point to you is I would hope that our position is to strengthen the effect of the sanctions today so that we have the very best chance to make diplomacy work and that we have an understanding with the international community, our partners in this, that they will also move to strengthen the sanctions. And yes, we are prepared to give you additional tools here in Congress. We would like to do that with you.

And I think Senator Corker's point about that is clear, Senator Menendez's point. I think you have the support of Congress. But I would hope that we could have a sense of urgency with our coalition partners on the sanctions to tighten the enforcements of these sanctions. How is our coalition responding to this? Are we making progress?

Ambassador SHERMAN. Thank you very much, Senator.

I do think we have made enormous progress. In every single meeting that we had at the U.N. General Assembly, and I think probably some of you saw the ''60 Minutes'' piece on Secretary Kerry. He had 59 bilateral meetings last week in the U.N. General Assembly, and I do not know how many I had on my own as well.

So in every single one of them where there was a concern about whether it was financial sanctions or oil sanctions or evaders, Iran was a topic of conversation. In virtually every one where it was relevant to that particular country, whether that was China, whether that was Russia, whether that was Turkey, whether that was India, whether it was to Indonesia—anybody that is part of that international coalition. Because you are quite right, what matters here is not——

Senator CARDIN. But China——

Ambassador SHERMAN [continuing]. Is that international group.

Senator CARDIN. China is still buying a significant amount of oil from Iran. Some of our closest allies in Asia are buying oil from

Iran. We have a ''Rebalance to Asia.'' It seems to me that we could be more effective in having greater help from those countries.

Ambassador SHERMAN. I agree. Indeed, as you know, Secretary Kerry is on his way to APEC and the East Asia summit. He is in Tokyo today. Iran is a big topic of conversation in Japan.

If the President is able to go to APEC and to the East Asia summit—he is not going to Malaysia and the Philippines—Iran will be a big topic of conversation as well. There are talking points that are part of any bilaterals held there to make sure we move forward.

Senator CARDIN. And those talking points are to strengthen the enforcements?

Ambassador SHERMAN. It is to ensure the enforcement, to strengthen the enforcement, to watch what Iran does on the 15th and 16th. Many of these countries have a relationship with Iran. We do not. And so, one of our talking points is to say to them here is a message we want you to deliver to Iran.

This is the opportunity on the 15th and the 16th to put in front of the international community—not just the United States—in front of the international community, specific, concrete, substantive, and verifiable steps that will address the concerns of the international community. Take this opportunity, or you will see that pressure continuing to increase.

Senator CARDIN. Thank you.

The CHAIRMAN. Senator Risch.

Senator RISCH. Thank you, Mr. Chairman.

First of all, Mr. Chairman, let me say that I am glad you included Pastor Saeed Abedini, who is one of my constituents who is held in Iran, and the other two individuals. And frankly, without those people being freed, there is no chance that Iran is going to convince me that they have any willingness to participate in the international community and do what is right here.

Secondly, let me say that I associate myself with the remarks of the chairman and with Senator Cardin, and we have had some discussions here about the shutdown, and I think the world knows that we are having an intramural fight here over internal policy. But let there be no mistake. When it comes to these kinds of issues, we stand shoulder to shoulder on them, and we are not divided on these issues. We will move forward together on these issues as Americans and will join the country.

Given that, let me say that I appreciate Senator Cardin's remarks, and again, I know this gets into the political weeds, and I cannot speak for all Republicans. But if a bill came to the floor in moments that relieved our intelligence services, the State Department enforcing these sanctions, and all the problems that you have described, I would vote for it in a heartbeat. And although I cannot speak for any other Republicans, I can tell you that I think it would probably, if we had a vote on it, pass the Senate unanimously.

But we are not going to get a vote on it for political reasons, and it is unfortunate. But I want you to know that I am there, and I think most every Republican, if not all Republicans, would be there to back the expenditure of those funds because we all agree on that. And it is really unfortunate that those of us that have been elected to govern and want to govern cannot govern because we cannot get a vote on these things.

So we are going to continue to work on it. We know what is right for the country, and this has got to get resolved.

Let me move for a minute to the new President of Iran. Frankly, I have been really dismayed by the embracement of this charm offensive that he brought to the United States. When you look at this man's history, and indeed, when you look at his abilities, when we all know who is actually running that country, we ought to just flat ignore him. He has indicated that he has used this type of tactic in the past to achieve the policies and the goals that Iran wants to achieve in the nuclear field.

And so, having said that, what can we expect of him now? What we can expect is the front that he is putting on, the facade that he is putting on, is to do exactly what he has been doing all along, including in formal meetings, that he bamboozled us. And he brags about bamboozling us.

And look, we are smarter than this. We should understand that this guy, what he is saying now, you cannot put any weight on whatsoever when you look at what his history is. So I, for one, have been very disappointed at all of this.

I think what we ought to do is take a step back and say, look, we do not want to hear this stuff. We do not want to see smiles. We do not even want handshakes. What we want to see is some action. And I look forward to October 15. I would like to say that I had cautious optimism. I have no optimism.

I think what you are going to get is you are going to get another dog-and-pony show. I think you are going to get another shuffle, and I think it is going to be business as usual. And we have seen it day after day, month after month, year after year, while I have been here, and I think it is just going to go on until they can achieve what they want to achieve.

So bless you for what you do. Keep it up. You have a very difficult task, and I think this committee and this Congress is willing to help and willing to put our foot down firmly to proceed with the road we have gone down to try to bring these people to where they need to be.

Thank you.

Thank you, Mr. Chairman.

The CHAIRMAN. Thank you, Senator.

Senator Shaheen.

Senator SHAHEEN. Thank you, Mr. Chairman.

And thank you to Secretary Sherman. We very much appreciate your being here.

You talked a few minutes ago and in your testimony about meaningful, transparent, and verifiable steps that would address core issues. I want to ask you, first, if there is agreement within the administration about what those concrete, verifiable steps would look like in order for negotiations to continue?

And then, secondly, whether there is agreement with our international partners about what those steps should look like?

Ambassador SHERMAN. Thank you very much, Senator.

We have extensive discussions about various scenarios before we go to a negotiation, both internally and with our P5+1 partners, because it is being united that really makes any negotiation effective. And doing a negotiation with six partners is never an easy undertaking.

And as Senator Cardin and others have pointed out, it is the international unity of sanctions and the international unity of negotiations that makes this effective. And if there are divisions, it makes it much harder. So, yes, we have gotten clear about where we want to head at the end of the day, what might be an early test of whether there is anything real here, and we, in fact, have many mechanisms in advance of the negotiation to make sure that we are completely united in our approach.

And you know, we may disagree with some of our partners in the P5+1 on many things. Russia and China do not always agree with us. Some of my European partners sometimes want to go further than I want to go. But at the end of the day, we come to an agreement because we all understand how important it is to be united in going forward, and I appreciate, as Senator Risch says, the bipartisanship on this issue.

I did, if I may, Senator, want to make one remark in response to Senator Risch, which goes to this as well. The shutdown and putting a piece of legislation on for the intelligence community or for OFAC at Treasury would, indeed, be helpful. But it would not be nearly enough. There are so many parts of this that are problematic.

Even in the State Department, indeed, 2014 security assistance funding for Israel, for instance, will be delayed until there is a CR or full-year appropriation. Our ability to protect the Sinai is delayed with that force.

So no one piece of legislation is going to solve what is a very complex international issue that we face, and we are beginning to see editorials, which we understand they are political. So we only take them so far.

But in Sri Lanka, where we have been pressing them very hard on democracy, governance, and human rights, they wrote a very critical editorial today, you know, saying health care is a universal human right, and yet the United States cannot come to an agreement on it. So who are they to preach to us about accountability and governance?

So this is very complicated for us, but I very much appreciate the bipartisan support on Iran and our efforts to move this forward.

Thank you.

Senator SHAHEEN. Thank you.

I would just have one disagreement with you, and that is I think there is one piece of legislation that would deal with this. And all the Speaker has to do is to call it up, and that would get us a continuing resolution that would keep the Government open.

But let me just go back to your statement because I understood you to say that there are ongoing negotiations. It was not clear to me whether you were saying that there is agreement now on how those negotiations might go forward and what people are looking for from those.

Ambassador SHERMAN. We are finalizing what the negotiation frame will look like. What I will say is that the P5+1 has agreed that the proposal we put on the table in Almaty stays on the table, and we will not offer anything new in the first instance. The onus is on Iran to put their response on the table to us.

So we are waiting to hear from Foreign Minister Zarif, who will head the delegation. We will not put new ideas on the table until we hear from Iran.

Senator SHAHEEN. Thank you.

I only have a few seconds left, but I was struck by the news accounts of Rouhani's return to Iran and that there were demonstrators there in opposition to him and to some of his statements. And I wonder if you could speak to the internal situation in Iran and to what extent he continues to have the support of the religious leaders in the country.

Ambassador SHERMAN. Well, as many of your colleagues have pointed out, Rouhani is very much part of the religious cleric class in Iran. He has been a member of the Expediency Discernment Council. He has been on the Supreme National Security Council. So he is very close to the Supreme Leader.

He is very tough. He is very conservative. But he does have politics, even in Iran. He won as a moderate—moderate in their system, not moderate in our system. But he won as a moderate in their system, saying that he would take a different approach to the West.

But he does have to deal with people who are much more hardline than he is. Hard-liner that he is, there are people who are more hard-line.

I would suspect that those protesters were approved by the regime so that we would see that there was not just support for what Rouhani was doing, there were also some people who opposed what Rouhani was doing. And I think the Supreme Leader has given Rouhani and Zarif enough rope to get this over the line and perhaps even enough rope for other purposes if they are not successful.

Senator SHAHEEN. Thank you very much.

The CHAIRMAN. Senator Rubio.

Senator RUBIO. Thank you, Mr. Chairman.

Thank you for being here today, Madam Secretary.

This is not a new issue for our country. Back in the 1990s, I know you were involved with President Clinton in the North Korean experience. At the time, President Clinton was adamant that North Korea would not attain a nuclear capability, and of course, they did.

And I raise that for the following question that I have, and let me preface it with this. There are five countries in the world that enrich uranium or reprocess plutonium, but they do not have a weapon. Those countries are Germany, Japan, Brazil, Argentina, and the Netherlands.

Then there are two other countries that enrich or reprocess, but do have a weapon—North Korea and Pakistan.

So my first question is which one of these two types of countries does Iran look like the most? Do they look more like North Korea and Pakistan, or do they look more like Germany and Japan and Brazil and Argentina? Who do they resemble the most?

Ambassador SHERMAN. Senator, I would make a couple comments. One, they resemble themselves. They are a sui generis case, in many ways more dangerous than any country who has the ability to reprocess, enrich, or has nuclear weapons or seeks to get nuclear weapons.

Senator RUBIO. Okay, but——

Ambassador SHERMAN [continuing]. So——

Senator RUBIO [continuing]. I understand they have a special case. They are only different in some ways than North Korea and Pakistan, but I think you would agree they do not look anything like Germany, Japan, Brazil, Argentina, or the Netherlands.

Ambassador SHERMAN. Of course not.

Senator RUBIO. Okay. Here is why I am asking that. The President, at the U.N. General Assembly, he said that we respect the right of the Iranian people to "access peaceful nuclear energy." And that sounds innocuous enough.

Now the President of Iran has said publicly that Iran's right to enrichment is nonnegotiable. So here is my question, what is our position? What is our official position? Does Iran have a right to enrich plutonium—to enrich uranium or to reprocess plutonium?

Ambassador SHERMAN. So the President's full comment on the quote that you gave is, "I have made clear we respect the right of the Iranian people to access peaceful nuclear energy in the context of Iran meeting its obligations. So the test will be meaningful, transparent, and verifiable actions which can also bring relief from the comprehensive international sanctions that are currently in place."

So the President has circumscribed what he means by the Iranian people having access, and that word was, as National Security Adviser Rice said on Fareed Zakaria, very carefully chosen. Access, not right. But access to peaceful nuclear energy in the context of meeting its obligations.

Senator RUBIO. So, is it our position that Iran has the right to have access to uranium or plutonium for peaceful purposes, but they do not have a right to enrich it or reprocess it themselves? Is that our position?

Ambassador SHERMAN. It has always been the United States position—and I have said to my Iranian interlocutors many times—is that article 4 of the Nuclear Nonproliferation Treaty does not speak about the right of enrichment at all; does not speak to enrichment, period.

It simply says that you have a right to research and development, and many countries, including countries like Japan and Germany, have taken that to be a right. But the United States does not take that position. We take the position that we look at each one of these.

And more to the point, the U.N. Security Council resolution has suspended Iran's enrichment until they meet their international obligations. They did not say they have suspended their right to enrichment. They have suspended their enrichment.

So we do not believe there is an inherent right by anyone to enrichment.

Senator RUBIO. Okay, so no one has an inherent right to enrichment, although you have outlined the case of these countries, which, by your own admission, they do not resemble Iran at all.

So, as we enter negotiations with Iran, why is that not our starting point? Why do we not make that very clear? Because the President of Iran has made it very clear that in his opinion, enrichment is nonnegotiable. Why does not our President say, as he has said on other issues that we are facing now as a country, that he will not negotiate until a certain condition is met?

He has laid down those markers on some domestic disputes that we are having now. So why doesn't he enter the negotiation with Iran by simply saying there is no negotiation until you give up your enrichment and your reprocessing capability because of the kind of country that you are, as you have described?

Ambassador SHERMAN. It is very interesting, Senator. I think it was today or yesterday that President Rouhani actually qualified his own statement. He said we will not give up our capability to have enrichment, but we can discuss the details.

So, you know, a negotiation begins with everybody having their maximalist position, and we have ours, too, which is they have to meet all of their obligations under the NPT and the U.N. Security Council resolutions. And they have their maximalist positions, and then you begin a negotiation.

Senator RUBIO. Here is my last question then, Will President Obama ever agree to ease sanctions in any negotiation that does not require Iran to abandon its enrichment and reprocessing capabilities?

Ambassador SHERMAN. I am not going to negotiate in public, Senator, with all due respect. All I can do is repeat what the President of the United States has said, which is we respect the right of the Iranian people to access peaceful nuclear energy in the context of Iran meeting its obligations. The test will be meaningful, transparent, and verifiable actions.

Senator RUBIO. Okay. So my last question then is you are not able to say here today that there will never be an agreement to lower sanctions so long as Iran does not abandon its enrichment or its reprocessing capabilities?

Ambassador SHERMAN. What I can say to you today is that Iran must meet the concerns of the international community, including the United States, and all of its obligations under the NPT and the U.N. Security Council resolutions, which have suspended its enrichment.

The CHAIRMAN. Senator Coons.

Senator COONS. Thank you, Chairman Menendez. Thank you for convening this critically important hearing and ensuring that this committee continues to fulfill its constitutional duty, even in the middle of a Government shutdown.

And Madam Secretary, thank you and to all the witnesses who will appear today. And thank you for the very hard work that you and the Secretary have been doing to continue to strengthen and sustain the sanctions regime, which is critical to getting some chance of some progress in this.

In engagement with Iran, we have to be clear-eyed and realistic about our goals. And at the end of the day, I think there is broad agreement here that we must not allow Iran to acquire nuclear weapons capability and that any negotiations must demand a verifiable end to their uranium enrichment program.

I support the President's assertion that all options are on the table. I appreciate your opening comment about the actions of this committee and its role in progress with regards to Syria, and I strongly believe that the credible threat of military force has to be maintained in order that there be any progress around the negotiating table.

I am encouraged, frankly, that the sanctions are having some real impact, both in terms of economic repercussions and, hopefully, forcing the regime in Iran to change its calculus with regards to their nuclear program. That has formed, I think, the basis for negotiations. But I also think it is unclear whether Hassan Rouhani is genuine in his stated intentions and is capable of making a deal.

So I might also say at the outset I appreciate your continuing to press the cases of several Americans or Iranian Americans. In my case, I have been concerned about and engaged with the case of Mr. Hekmati. This charm offensive to me is so far not charming. The release of political dissidents and prisoners is a beginning and very, very modest step and could be advanced further by taking real steps to end the oppression within Iran and ongoing terrorist actions outside of Iran to kill or take hostage Iranian dissidents.

So let us talk, if we could, first about whether or not Rouhani is capable of making a deal. Does he have the authority from the Supreme Leader? Khamenei in a speech in September talked about heroic flexibility. But I was pleased to hear you clear-eyed about the fact that deception, as I think you said, has long been part of the DNA of their negotiating strategy.

Does Rouhani have the authority to make a real deal and see it through?

Ambassador SHERMAN. I think we do not know, Senator, to be perfectly honest. He says he has a mandate from the Supreme Leader to—as does Foreign Minister Zarif, in a derivative fashion—to, in fact, come to an agreement with the international community. But as I have said, we are ready to test that, but we do not know, and he may not know.

It may be that the Supreme Leader has said to President Rouhani and Foreign Minister Zarif, ''Go give it a try. See where you can go, see where you can get.'' And they may not even know what the limitations are of their ability to negotiate. But we have to test this, and we have to test it, as many of your colleagues have said, in a short enough period of time, in a way to ensure that their nuclear program cannot just go on and on and on and on and on to a point where we wake up one day and find out they have the capability we all do not want them to have.

So we will test this. We will do it in a relatively short period of time. We will see if there is anything real here, and we will see whether President Rouhani, Foreign Minister Zarif can deliver on what they have said to us, which is they not only have a mandate from the Iranian people, but a mandate from the Supreme Leader. But we have to test it.

Senator COONS. Well, we have short timelines, I think, both in terms of their steady progress, their steady advancement toward a nuclear capability and this shutdown.

This maddening, I think unconstructive, destructive shutdown of the U.S. Federal Government, as you mentioned at the outset, is preventing both OFAC and the intelligence community from effectively enforcing sanctions.

What is the plan forward for dealing with this shutdown, should it continue for another couple of weeks? And how do we make sure that the American people understand the very real risk this is creating for the United States and for our goals with regards to stopping Iran's work toward a nuclear weapons capability?

Ambassador SHERMAN. Well, I certainly think, Senator, that this hearing today, the statements from the members, from the Senators, helps to convey that message. I think it is critical that we move forward in the bipartisan way that this committee has proceeded to deal with Iran, and to do so, we not only need all of the tools at our disposal to enforce the sanctions. But we need all of the tools at our disposal for national security and foreign policy, including the lectures that we give to countries all over the world about good governance.

I have been in Washington for a very long time and once worked up here on Capitol Hill. I know that Members on both sides of the aisle can come to the right decision, and we are all hopeful—I speak as an American citizen now—that that happens very quickly.

Senator COONS. Well, last, if I might, you know, Rouhani has made all these great promises, both at the United Nations, but also domestically. What, if any, evidence is there that the human rights situation within Iran has improved or that Iran has in any way backed off their campaign against Iranian dissidents outside of Iran?

What more could we be doing to try and advance human rights, both within Iran or to thwart their efforts outside of Iran that have taken many lives and have continued to threaten stability regionally?

Ambassador SHERMAN. Thank you, Senator.

As you said, we welcomed the release of 16 prisoners of conscience, including human rights lawyer Nasrin Sotoudeh. But we hope that Iran will expeditiously free all of the 80 political prisoners whose pardons it recently announced, many of whom we are still working to confirm as released.

So, indeed, it would be very, very wise of Iran to speak to the international community by making affirmation of the release of all of those prisoners.

In addition, as you pointed out, we have three Americans that we are all quite concerned about—Robert Levinson, Amir Hekmati, and Saeed Abedini. Both Mr. Hekmati and Mr. Abedini are in prison. It would be a grand humanitarian gesture, since they really did nothing wrong, for them to be released, and it would be very, very important if Robert Levinson, who has not been known to his family since March 2007, almost 7 years now—almost 7 years—for Iran to cooperate, help us to find out where he is and get him released back to his family.

Finally, we have sanctioned more than 30 Iranian individuals and organizations for their involvement or complicity in serious human rights abuses and censorship. We will continue to move in that regard on sanctions enforcement. We have continued to strongly support the mandate of the U.N. special rapporteur for human rights in Iran, and we also use our Virtual Embassy Tehran platform and its associated USAdarFarsi Facebook, YouTube, Twitter, and Google+ platforms to promote freedom of expression, respect for human rights, and free and fair and transparent electoral processes.

It is very interesting that Alan Eyre, who is a fluent Farsi speaker and really the voice of our face to Iranians, an interview with him was put on the front page of an Iranian paper for the first time, including with a very nice picture of Alan. He is part of our delegation and our team for negotiations because he is a fluent Farsi speaker.

He understands Iran quite well. It helps to understand sometimes what is going on in the room. So he is a great asset on all of these issues.

The CHAIRMAN. Senator Johnson.

Senator COONS. Thank you, Mr. Chairman.

Senator JOHNSON. Thank you, Mr. Chairman. And I would like to thank the chairman for making the determination that this hearing was essential to our continuing the government here.

I happen to think that national security is the top priority of government. I think it is actually an essential part of government, and so I would also like to thank Secretary Sherman for coming here today. I am thankful the State Department has certainly determined that you are essential as we are moving forward to making sure that we enforce the sanctions against Iran because that is essential to our national security.

So let me start with that; that question. I appreciate the fact that in your testimony, you said that the shutdown is causing concern about our being able to enforce Iran sanctions. So does not the State Department, does not the Treasury Department have the ability, just like we have in Congress, of making a determination in terms of what is essential activity?

Ambassador SHERMAN. Well, certainly. And the head of OFAC, I understand, I think is still at work, as well as with a couple of staff. But OFAC's responsibilities are enormous, and they have to determine, given what they have in front of them, who they can keep and who they cannot.

Senator JOHNSON. But we are here today in this hearing because we believe the actions of Iran pose a serious national security threat to this Nation. So why would the State Department or the Treasury Department not deem the people in charge of enforcing the sanctions against Iran as an essential service of the Federal Government? Why would they not do that?

Ambassador SHERMAN. Well, we only have limited budgets available to us. So I know that you would believe that there are many things that Treasury must do to make sure that U.S. currency, U.S. monetary and fiscal policy is protected. I mean, they have a whole variety of things that are essential to U.S. national security and foreign policy and economy——

Senator JOHNSON. It is a matter of prioritizing spending.

Ambassador SHERMAN. Well, it is not just a matter of prioritizing spending. There are bottom lines here, Senator, with all due respect. And I think the fundamental point here is, I truly believe every member of this committee wants us to keep Iran front and center, as we do.

And I know that Secretary Lew, I know that DNI Clapper and Director Brennan all want to make sure that Iran is front and center. But there are realities to how much money we have available to us during the shutdown.

Senator JOHNSON. Okay. Well——

Ambassador SHERMAN. And it is limited.

Senator JOHNSON. Well, Madam Secretary, as I said to you before the hearing, I really would like to think that we can have politics end at the water's edge. And I believe this committee really has shown that capability I think during a very thoughtful debate on the Syrian issue. So I believe that is true.

But then you come before the committee here, and I think very appropriately, again, I appreciate the fact that you are pointing out to us that you are concerned about our ability to enforce the sanctions against Iran. So I guess the question I would have is, is it not also appropriate then for you to come before Congress, maybe before the House and say, listen, if you do not have the ability to deem those sanction enforcers as essential, if you need additional funding, to ask the House to pass a measure quickly, which I believe they would do probably today if you made the request.

And then ask Senator Harry Reid to bring that up in front of the Senate. Probably on the basis of unanimous consent, I think we could get that funding to you in a matter of hours. I mean, would you be willing to work with Congress to do just that?

Ambassador SHERMAN. As I said——

Senator JOHNSON. Because it is essential.

Ambassador SHERMAN. As I said, Senator, I believe that there are many essential pieces to what we do. Many.

Senator JOHNSON. Have you made the point to the President how crucial it is to make sure that we maintain the sanctions and can enforce them against Iran? Have you made that point to the President?

Ambassador SHERMAN. I think that everyone knows that it is essential that we enforce things with Iran. I also believe that it is essential that we make sure that Israel's peace and security is affirmed through our budget. I also believe that it is essential that we can, in fact, talk with countries around the world about good governance and have credibility when we do so because our own system is working.

Senator JOHNSON. Okay.

Ambassador SHERMAN. So this is very complicated, and I defer to the bipartisanship up here to ultimately solve the problem. You know how better to get that done than I do.

Senator JOHNSON. Well, obviously, we are at an impasse right here, and discussions are not working very well. I certainly did not want to have a Government shutdown. But now we are having the House making the attempt to start passing over—let us call them—mini appropriation bills.

The way the process ought to work, it should have happened months ago. But again, I am highly concerned about the national security of this Nation. I would hope the President is equally concerned.

So that being the case, we are at this impasse. Why do we not at least allow the House to pass mini appropriation bills, mini continuing resolutions, so we can fund the essential parts of Government so that we are not concerned about the enforcement of the sanctions against Iran?

Again, I would really encourage you through the administration, talking to the President, whoever you need to talk to, to make that request, allow that to come to a vote in the Senate and have President Obama sign those funding measures so that we can continue with the essential services of Government.

Thank you.

The CHAIRMAN. Senator Kaine.

Senator KAINE. Mr. Chair, I was not going to do this, but I cannot resist. It is not the Department of State's fault, and it is not the administration's fault that Congress has not passed a budget.

It is not the Department of State's fault, and it is not the administration's fault that the House and some in this body have repeatedly blocked even a budget conference from starting. Everyone around this table knows this, but just for folks who are here. The Senate had not passed a budget in 4 years, and we passed one on the 23rd of March, the same week that the House passed a budget.

And we have been making an effort to go into a budget conference so that we can make these funding decisions since the 23rd of March and have been blocked in doing it 19 times. The attitude has been we will not have a budget conference because we are not interested in talking. We are not interested in listening. We are not interested in compromise.

Only after pushing the Government to shutdown at midnight Monday did the House say, well, now let us have a conference. But not a conference about the budget. Let us have a conference about whether or not the Government of the United States should be open or closed.

I mean, we should not be expecting the State Department to help bail Congress out of the dysfunction of not being willing to sit down and compromise. I mean, please, do all you can to stress the critical nature of your work, but we know that, and so does the President. This is up to Congress to solve, and it is only going to get solved if we sit down and have a conference about the budget, which we have been trying to do since March.

Now my question, it is really an observation, and it is based upon some questions that I have heard Senator Risch ask before. Ambassador Sherman, in the sanctions regime against Iran, an area that I continue to be concerned about, is the waivers to nations that continue to purchase Iranian oil in a significant way. And Senator Risch and I were in a hearing recently with an Ambassador candidate to India, and we were talking about that or who is going to deal with India.

And the nations and especially China, which purchases such a large amount, that continue to purchase Iranian oil, if we could get them to do more to scale back their energy purchases, I think it would take the sanctions regime, which are having an effect, and make them even more effective and, hopefully, help us.

We had a meeting in early July, and I think Senator McCain was at this meeting. Senator Reid pulled it together. It was with the number-two leader of the Chinese Government, and I asked him this question. You have reduced your oil purchases from Iran for a variety of reasons, including to help the sanctions. Could you reduce them dramatically further and then say, but if you give up your nuclear program, we are going to buy a lot more from you?

So have a stick, but then have a carrot. And could India do the same thing? Dramatically reduce oil purchases, but with a carrot down the road. Or Japan could do the same thing.

And the response of the Chinese official was very adroit and very quick. He said we would be very willing to consider cutting our purchases from Iran even further if you would sell us liquid natural gas.

Now that was the issue we were talking about with our Ambassador or representatives to India. And I would just kind of, from a political affairs standpoint, hope that the United States asset, this significant supply of natural gas, while the exportation of it has some other domestic economic issues we ought to balance, I think that is a real resource and asset that we could have that could even take the nations that we are currently exempting from the sanctions and could help them dramatically reduce their purchases in a short-term period as a way to enhance sanctions.

And I just want to sort of encourage you to think about that asset in that way.

Ambassador SHERMAN. Thank you very much, Senator.

Indeed, our energy bureau, headed up by Ambassador Pascual, has looked very carefully at this and be glad to ask him to come up and brief the committee on what we are doing in this regard. LNG works in some countries as a substitute. In others, it does not.

And as you point out, there are a lot of domestic as well as international issues involved in deciding whether we are going to export our gas and the tremendous asset we have now discovered that we have. But I do think it is something worth pursuing. We are pursuing it and would be glad to arrange a briefing for the committee on what works about this and what does not work about this and how we could move it forward and what are the considerations for it.

We also agree that we need to keep pressing China. India, Turkey, South Korea, Japan, and their small amounts of oil that still go to Taiwan, that we need to keep pressing, and we are, all of them, for reductions. But all 23 importers of Iranian oil have either eliminated or significantly reduced purchases from Iran, and we are left with only 5 major customers of oil.

So, with your help, thank you for the tremendous progress.

Senator KAINE. And Mr. Chairman. Mr. Chairman, if I might just very quickly?

But you continue to believe, though, that if those five major purchasers continued to scale back in significant ways, that could be a very strong additional leverage point to increase sanctions and help us with our diplomatic discussions surrounding the Iranian nuclear program?

Ambassador SHERMAN. Without a doubt. Though I would note, particularly probably for China and India, it becomes more and more difficult to do because their demands are growing exponentially even as they are reducing. And I think I have used this statistic in front of the committee before.

A given percentage reduction from China, who is currently the largest purchaser of oil from Iran, would be approximately equal to a volume reduction twice as large as the same percentage reduction from India, three times as large as the same percentage reduction from South Korea, and four times bigger than the same percentage reduction from Turkey.

So even a 1-percent decline in Chinese purchases is double what anybody else's reduction is because their volumes are so great.

The CHAIRMAN. Senator McCain.

Senator MCCAIN. Thank you, Mr. Chairman.

Thank you, Secretary Sherman. Thank you for being here.

I think there is a question in the minds of many of us about credibility. Mr. Rouhani is one of the most trusted figures of the Islamic regime's Supreme Leader. He has been the Deputy Speaker of Parliament, and as we know, he also served as a negotiator.

And then, on an interview that he gave, which is out there on the Internet, ''The day that we invited the three European ministers, only 10 centrifuges were spinning at the Iranian nuclear facility.'' Rouhani boasted on the tape, ''We could not produce one gram of U4 or U6. We did not have the heavy water production. We could not produce yellow cake. Our total production of centrifuges inside the country was 150.''

But then Rouhani admitted in the video the purpose of prolonging negotiations. ''We wanted to complete all of these. We needed time.'' He said three European ministers promised to block U.S. efforts to transfer the Iranian nuclear dossier to the United Nations using veto power as necessary.

He called Iran's claim that it stopped its nuclear program in 2003 a statement for the uneducated and admitted that the program not only continued, but it was significantly expanded under his tenure. In the interview, Rouhani said that after he took over the country's nuclear project, the country's 150 grew to 1,700 by the time he left the project.

Then Rouhani made his boldest statement. ''We did not stop. We completed the program.''

Now we are supposed to trust this guy? What possible confidence do you have in this individual?

Ambassador SHERMAN. Senator, I do not trust the people who sit across the table from me in these negotiations, and you are quite right that Rouhani was the chief negotiator from 2003, 2005, and I am well familiar with that interview with his book. That as Secretary Kerry has said, we must test the proposition that has been put before us, but not forever and ever, for the reasons you point out.

Senator MCCAIN. How long should the test take, do you think?

Ambassador SHERMAN. Well, I think we will know whether we are even at the beginning——

Senator MCCAIN. So we do not know how long the test will take?

Ambassador SHERMAN. We will know——

Senator MCCAIN. Do you have a date?

Ambassador SHERMAN. Can I finish my sentence?

Senator MCCAIN. Sure.

Ambassador SHERMAN. Thank you, Senator.

I think we will know when we meet on the 15th and 16th whether there is anything real here or not. I think we will know rather quickly whether we are beginning a serious negotiation or whether we are moving down one more road that leads nowhere.

Senator MCCAIN. Do we have evidence that the Iranian regime is training their regular forces in the use of chemical weapons in Syria?

Ambassador SHERMAN. In this setting, what I can say to you, Senator, is that we are quite well aware that Iran is very heavily engaged in Syria, both with advisers, boots on the ground, the financing of Lebanese Hezbollah, providing all kinds of strategic advice in ways that are quite destructive and horrific.

Senator MCCAIN. So you cannot say in public hearing whether we know whether the Iranians are training Syrians in the use of chemical weapons or not?

Ambassador SHERMAN. I will be glad to have our intelligence community come back to you on that.

Senator MCCAIN. I see. Is Qasem Soleimani playing a role in the Assad regime's decisionmaking, in your assessment? What influence does he have over the regime's command and control?

Ambassador SHERMAN. What I can say, again, in this setting, and I think we probably should make sure we get a classified briefing for you on all of this, Qasem Soleimani is very critical to the IRGC Quds Force. He is engaged, we believe, in what is going on in Syria in ways that obviously we wish he was not.

Senator MCCAIN. And the situation, as a result, to the Camp Ashraf people. We know they were Iranian dissidents. At one point, they were designated as a terrorist organization. But the United States of America, is it true, gave them an assurance that if they moved, that they would be protected?

We know the Iranian influence has dramatically increased in Iraq. In fact, we know now that al-Qaeda is alive and well and doing extremely well, moving back and forth across the two countries. Now, there was a murder of, I believe, 51 people who were members of this camp, and many of them had in their possession guarantees from the United States of America that they would not be harmed.

First of all, are those facts true? And second of all, if true, what lesson does that send to people who we say will be under our protection?

Ambassador SHERMAN. Senator, I share your deep concern about what happened at Camp Ashraf. This was a vicious attack on September 1, and many lives were lost. And the United States continues to press the Government of Iraq at every opportunity at the most senior levels to ensure the safety and security of residents at Camp Hurriya, where many of the MEK were moved for better safety.

We strongly and swiftly condemned the attack. We, of course, extend our condolences to the victims' families, and we are working with the Government of Iraq and the United Nations Assistance Mission for Iraq, UNAMI, to peacefully and voluntarily transfer the surviving residents to safety at Camp Hurriya on September 12.

And we are working for the protection of the people in Camp Hurriya because we do not want a repeat of this.

So, to date, the Government of Iraq has moved in over 700 large T-walls, over 500 bunkers, over 600 small T-walls, and nearly 50,000 sandbags. U.N. monitors visit the camp daily, in accordance with the MOU, to assess human rights and humanitarian conditions.

But I must say, Senator, the real answer to this, to the safety and security of all of the people in the camps—who wants to live in a camp?—is resettlement to third countries to get out of Iraq and to get out of harm's way. And I would call on all of the people who are here today representing the rights and interests of the MEK and the leaders of the MEK in the camps and in Paris to allow this resettlement to go forward because until the resettlement happens, safety and security is going to be at risk.

We will do everything in our power to keep people safe in these camps. But as you point out, the al-Qaeda threat is increasing in Iraq, and it is difficult.

Senator MCCAIN. Unfortunately, we did not keep our word, despite your good words, and I appreciate those good words. And I hope that—and I hope that this issue will be raised with the Iraqi Government, and we in Congress may have to look at the kind of aid and how we are extending that to Iraq if this kind of thing is going to be countenanced by the Iraqi Government.

And I do not—I used up all my time. I thank you for your response.

The CHAIRMAN. Before I turn to Senator Markey, let me echo what Senator McCain has said in this regard, and I have put out a statement in this regard. I have also talked to our department. You know, America went to the MEK, and we said disarm and we will protect you. And then we ultimately left, and that protection has not been there.

You can put up I do not care how many tons of sandbags, but when elements of the Iranian—excuse me, of the Iraqi forces actually may very well be complicit in what took place, sandbags are not going to take care of the problem. And I agree with you that resettlement is a critical part. Maybe the United States could be part of leading the way in saying to a universe of these individuals that, in fact, you can be resettled to the United States, and that would get the rest of the world to offer further resettlement.

But it is unacceptable to lose one more life when American commanders gave these individuals a written guarantee toward their safety, and it sends a message to others in the world that when we say that we are going to do that and we do not, that they should not trust us.

And for one thing that this committee can do, since it has jurisdiction over all weapons sales, is that I doubt very much that we are going to see any approval of any weapons sales to Iraq until we get this situation in a place in which people's lives are saved.

Senator Markey.

Senator MCCAIN. Could I say thank you, Mr. Chairman.

Senator MARKEY. The sanctions have squeezed the regime of Iran, but we cannot let the Iranians wriggle out of the impacts of the sanctions through a mirage of cooperation. We should not relax the sanctions one inch while Iran's intentions are still unknown.

And as you have noted, Madam Under Secretary, we are not in a trust, but verify situation with Iran here. We do not trust the Iranian regime, and we should not trust the Iranian regime. And that is where we are going to be, and I think we all agree on that.

There has been a very high historical prevarication coefficient coming out of Iran on this program. And by the way, they are no different than the North Koreans. They are no different than the Iraqis. They are no different than the Syrians. They were all using what each of these countries says is an interest in wattage, electricity wattage, in order to get access to a civilian nuclear electricity program to compromise it in order to obtain the uranium and plutonium.

They all lie. They all lie. It is all about the nuclear weapons. And each country does it, and we keep falling for it. Not ''we''—in general, the world keeps falling for it. We keep trusting them, you know, to not compromise it, and all you need is a slight change in the government, and all of a sudden, these materials are going into the hands of those that want a weapons program.

And by the way, that is my concern about saying, well, we will consider giving a nuclear program to Saudi Arabia or, for that matter, to the United Arab Emirates. When the government changes, so can the program as they just boot out all those people who were inspecting the civilian program.

It is just an ongoing storyline that never changes, and then we wind up getting deeper and deeper, which is why we have to be thankful for the Israelis in 1981 when they bombed the Osirak nuclear power plant in Iraq. It was not truly under full-scope safeguards. And when they bombed the Syrian nuclear plant, they did the world a favor because, again, this whole safeguards regime question is completely dependent upon how intrusive, how continuous the inspections regime is in guaranteeing that the program is not compromised.

And I do not think it should take a long time to determine whether or not they are going to allow the inspectors in to go to those sites to begin the preliminary work. We all know that is what happened in Iraq. They let the inspectors in when they thought there was going to be a war, and we could not find the nuclear weapon program, okay?

We should have never started the war because we could not find the program that was the ostensible justification to make sure the next attack did not come in the form of a mushroom cloud, and we could not find the program. But we had the inspectors in, and they were riding all over that country. That is what Iran has to accept.

There has been a compromise to this program, okay, as other countries have compromised their nuclear programs. And that is why we have to be very careful in the Middle East as we talk about Saudi Arabia having a civilian nuclear program. There are 300 days of sunshine in the Middle East. Whenever we are talking about selling nuclear power for electricity into countries that have oil and gas, okay, then we should just cast an arched eyebrow.

It is very, very likely that 10 years from now, 20, 30, it will all turn on us again, and we will be talking about American young men and women being put at risk. So I guess my question just came in the form of that comment. I would like to move over, if I could, very briefly over to the cyber issue.

We know that there are Iranian extremists that have been attacking sites in the United States, in Saudi Arabia, other places. What role is their capacity to launch cyber attacks on the West, on other countries in the Middle East, playing in these negotiations to make sure they know that we want that shut down as well, and we do not want them playing games in this ever-increasingly dangerous area of international conflict?

Ambassador SHERMAN. Senator, thank you. Thank you for your comments, and you have long been a leader and a champion and a speaker about nuclear energy, nuclear power, nuclear weapons. You and I have had these conversations for many years.

Where cyber is concerned, we are, of course, concerned about the capability of Iran. We are concerned about the capability of many countries in the world to use cyber.

Where Iran is specifically concerned, I think that discussion would better take place in a classified setting, and I would be glad to arrange for that briefing to occur.

Senator MARKEY. Well, again, I just want to say that that is a big part of this storyline.

Ambassador SHERMAN. Absolutely.

Senator MARKEY. Okay. And they use it, again, in a regional context that then drives these other countries toward their own sense that they have to increase their own protection. And so, I think it is absolutely critical that we play the lead role here.

Stuxnet played a big role right now in buying us more time, but we know that a counterpart capacity also exists in Iran and other countries to attack us, to attack the West, to attack those regional neighbors. And so, I just want to highlight that issue, thank you for your work on it, and wish you good luck. I think we are at a critical point.

And I would just say this in summation, Mr. Chairman. Back in the cold war, Brezhnev died, Chernenko died, Andropov died—three leaders in 3 years—and Gorbachev took over April of 1985. He said he wanted to end the nuclear arms race. He said he wanted to reduce nuclear arms. He said he wanted an agreement.

We had to test it, but we had a moral responsibility to test it and to trust, but verify, as Ronald Reagan said. We have a lot of reason to put Iran in the same category that we put the former Soviet Union. But Rouhani shows up as a new era potentially, potentially. And I think it is exactly what you just said. We do not know how long his leash is that the Supreme Leader is giving him.

But if it is one, then we can test it quickly because they can let those inspectors in, and we can get the preliminary guarantee that those sites are going to be made accessible to the world. And I think there will be a sigh of relief that will be breathed, as there was in the mid-1980s when Reagan was able to extract that same kind of inspection regimes.

I thank you, Mr. Chairman.

The CHAIRMAN. Thank you.

Madam Secretary, before we let you go, I have two final questions. One is last week Pakistan's Prime Minister said he intended to move forward with a natural gas pipeline deal with Iran that was agreed to by the previous government with Pakistan. If that were to take place, it would be in clear violation of our Iran sanctions regime, not to mention that it would provide a critical revenue stream to Iran, and it would create challenges globally with our other partners in terms of saying we are following you on the sanctions, but you cannot allow somebody to get away with it, and then all of us be ultimately subject to the sanctions.

Is the administration having discussions with Pakistan on this issue, and are we ready to proceed with sanctions if they continue on the deal?

Ambassador SHERMAN. Thank you, Mr. Chairman.

A couple of points, if I may? On Pakistan, we have those discussions and will continue with the Pakistani Government. My own assessment is it is not going anywhere anytime soon. But they certainly understand where we are and what our sanctions require, should it proceed.

So we will keep vigilant about not only what Pakistan may do, but any country that is going to have to confront the sanctions that the United States and the international community has at its disposal.

If I may, Senator, I would also like to take the opportunity to comment on what you said about Iraq. And we quite agree—and what Senator McCain said. We quite agree that we need to do everything we can to resettle the people, to get them out of the harm's way, to make good on the word we gave to the MEK.

I know that there are strong feelings up here, and I understand why, about arms sales to Iraq. But I do want to put on the record that U.S. security assistance and foreign military sales in particular are tools that we use for building and shaping Iraq's defense capabilities and integrating Iraqi security forces with our security forces and regional partners.

And I just want to caution that withholding security assistance may well serve to decrease our influence in Baghdad, cede relationships and leverage to strategic competitors who will fill the vacuum and could conceivably damage our long-term interests. So I just ask that we talk very carefully as we go forward.

The CHAIRMAN. Well, let me caution you about the overflights that Iraq has permitted from Iran into Syria largely with impunity. And let me also caution that the seven hostages, which we believe the Iraqi Government knows where they are, should they die, it would be complicating matters for all of that.

So I hope that we have both cautioned each other.

Ambassador SHERMAN. Quite agree. Quite agree. I quite agree with you on both issues.

The CHAIRMAN. Let me close by asking you one final question. What is it that we will accept less than what the world has said is necessary through the Security Council resolutions?

Ambassador SHERMAN. I am sorry?

The CHAIRMAN. What is it that we would accept in these negotiations with Iran less than what has been established under the Security Council resolutions?

Ambassador SHERMAN. We have continued to say to Iran that we expect them to fulfill all of their obligations under the NPT and the Security Council resolutions.

The CHAIRMAN. All right. Well, thank you for your testimony. I look forward to what the Department and the State Department is going to be able to do with Iran as you test their intentions. I intend to keep the Department's feet to the fire——

Ambassador SHERMAN. Thank you.

The CHAIRMAN [continuing]. On our issue of sanctions as we move forward. And Senator Corker.

Senator CORKER. Mr. Chairman, I will be very brief. I know we have another panel coming, but I would like to ask the Secretary. You know, we have talked a lot today about the nuclear issue and other important issues here today. But if we negotiate an end to their nuclear program or a significant rollback, we still have a country that is hostile.

They are a state sponsor of terror. They have a terrible human rights record. So, you know, I know that you all are looking at trying to negotiate some relief, if you will, relative to the sanctions. But the fact is that the way the sanctions law reads, they have got to not only dismantle their nuclear program, but they also have to renounce terrorism.

And I just wonder how are those negotiations going simultaneous to these others and what you are doing to ensure? Because, again, the way the law reads, these sanctions cannot be undone unless all of that occurs, and it seems to me we are only moving on one track, a very good one track. But I am just wondering how you might be addressing the other?

Ambassador SHERMAN. We have been clear with the Iranians that we are talking here about their nuclear program and the sanctions that relate to their nuclear program and that the sanctions that exist regarding human rights actions, their terrorist actions are still on the table because of exactly what you say, which is that they need to make progress, considerable progress around human rights. They have to stop their sponsorship of terrorism.

They have to stop regionally destabilizing that part of the world and many other parts of the world, quite frankly. So those are other discussions that we have with Iran, as is the subject of this today and as the subject of the 15th and 16th will be on their nuclear program.

Senator CORKER. Thank you.

The CHAIRMAN. Thank you, Madam Secretary, for your testimony. We always appreciate your service.

Ambassador SHERMAN. Thank you for the opportunity.

The CHAIRMAN. Let me call up our next panel. I have introduced them already, but David Albright, founder and president of the Institute for Science and International Security; the Honorable James F. Jeffrey, distinguished visiting fellow of the Washington Institute for Near East Peace, and Ray Takeyh, senior fellow for Middle East studies on the Council on Foreign Relations.

[Pause.]

The CHAIRMAN. And let me apologize to Mr. Takeyh for my mispronunciation of his name.

We welcome you. Your full testimony will be included in the record without objection. We ask you to summarize it in about 5 minutes or so, and we will start with Mr. Albright.

## STATEMENT OF DAVID ALBRIGHT, PRESIDENT, INSTITUTE FOR SCIENCE AND INTERNATIONAL SECURITY, WASHINGTON, DC

Dr. ALBRIGHT. Well, thank you very much, Mr. Chairman and Ranking Member Senator Corker and other members of the committee, for the opportunity to testify today.

I think it has been made clear that there is certainly hope that an agreement with Iran can be achieved over its nuclear program, and I think I certainly share many of the views here that one should be skeptical and move very quickly to test whether the Iranians have really changed.

And I think we also have to keep in mind that the goal is not necessarily specific limitations on their nuclear program, but it is to provide an agreement that ensures that they will not seek nuclear weapons. And I think that is a very difficult thing to do. And what I would like to do is talk through some of the issues on the nuclear program and then some of the implications of that kind of objective on what you would like to see in agreement.

And I think it is clear to everybody, and some have made this point today, that Iran's nuclear program is large and growing. And it is also true that there has been no signs of the reduction in that program since President Rouhani took office. In fact, some of his comments in New York clearly implied that he envisions a growing nuclear program.

And as you know, there are two main gas centrifuge sites in Natanz and Fordow. There is also growing suspicion that they may be building a new one, and President Rouhani has not provided answers to that question.

Also Iran has produced very large stocks of enriched uranium, significant stock that is near 20 percent enriched and then a very large stock of 3.5 percent enriched uranium. And then, during the last 2 years, Iran has essentially doubled the number of its centrifuges at Natanz and Fordow, and it now has over 19,000 centrifuges installed at these facilities. And 1,000 of them are these advanced centrifuges that we have worried about for years.

And so, Iran is putting together a considerable nuclear weapons production capability, if it chose to go that route. And I think, as I mentioned, in developing a negotiating position, we have to look at how to constrain that program and provide the kind of assurance we need that it would not build nuclear weapons, and in that, we have to consider how long it would take Iran to make weapon-grade uranium for a nuclear weapon.

And I think the chairman has mentioned some of the estimates, and we have done some looking at today and how much they could do. And essentially, if Iran made a decision today to produce weapon-grade uranium, which is, to us, the long pole in the tent of making a nuclear weapon, it could make enough weapon-grade uranium for a bomb in about 1 to 1.5 months.

Now there are many things that can happen that would lengthen that time, but that, to us, is a credible minimal time for Iran to break out. Now I do not think Iran would do that now because it would be detected by the inspectors, and it would have to fear that it would be struck militarily. So I think what we would call the breakout estimates provide some assurance that there is still some time to solve this problem.

But unfortunately, Iran continues to add centrifuges to its program, and we would hope that would stop. But if you look at the plan trends of its centrifuge program, we think that by mid-2014, Iran could have so many centrifuges installed and could also produce more 20 percent enriched uranium that it could break out before and break out and produce enough weapon-grade uranium for a bomb before the international inspectors could detect that.

Now that does not mean they would have a bomb at that time, and Ambassador Sherman talked about a U.S. estimate of about a year or up to a year. I mean, there is controversy on that. I think our estimate is to get an actual first nuclear explosive, it could take anywhere from 3 months to 12 months. We do not know their capabilities that well.

But in terms of the long pole in the tent, it is the weapon-grade uranium. And once they have enough for a bomb or two, it is going to change things fundamentally, even if it is going to take them several more months to actually construct a nuclear explosive. Therefore, negotiations should clearly aim to limit Iran's ability to reach what we call a critical capability and what you have called a breakout capability and to increase the time it takes Iran to build nuclear weapons.

Let me briefly talk about the plutonium side of this that I think Iran has caused more alarm by saying it is going to soon start the Iraq heavy water reactor, which, from a technical point of view, is pretty well designed to make weapon-grade plutonium and is not so well designed to make medical isotopes.

And so, there is worry that this could open a second pathway to nuclear weapons for Iran, if they operate it. And so, I think it is very important in negotiations to get Iran to first simply say we are not going to start it until 2015 or later and then to seek the end of this construction project and just eliminate this as a possibility.

Let me make one last point. For us, it is a very important one. We have worked on a lot of countries over time. We have seen countries get nuclear weapons. We have seen them give them up. One of the more troubling aspects of Iran's statements is its insistence that it had no nuclear weapons program in the past, it has none now, despite the overwhelming evidence that that is simply not true.

Now I understand, and Senator Markey made the point, countries often lie about their nuclear weapons programs. I mean, that is nothing new, and sometimes people live with those lies. But in the case of Iran, if they do not start opening up and I would say answering the questions of the International Atomic Energy Agency on this issue, which has well-developed evidence and a whole set of questions and a negotiating path with Iran to settle this—and unless they settle this, it is going to be very hard to believe anything they do on this question.

And I think if they are not willing to do this, then I am not sure they would pass the test that is needed to settle this issue.

Let me end there, and I apologize for going over.

[The prepared statement of Dr. Albright follows:]

PREPARED STATEMENT OF DR. DAVID ALBRIGHT

Iran has invested heavily in nuclear industries in the last 30 years. However, its investments, often made in secret and dominated by black market purchases, have not been consistent with a strictly peaceful nuclear program.

Despite many setbacks over the last three decades, Iran has found suppliers to provide the wherewithal to build many nuclear facilities. One of the most important suppliers was A.Q. Khan and his network of business associates in Europe, Asia, and Africa. They provided Iran in the 1980s and 1990s with many key requirements necessary to build and operate gas centrifuge plants. Without their assistance, Iran would have likely been unable to develop a successful gas centrifuge program. Since then, Iran has depended extensively on illicit foreign procurement of a wide range of nuclear-related dual-use goods to outfit many of its nuclear efforts. Those efforts continue today.

Iran's current nuclear infrastructure is large. It has two gas centrifuge sites, the underground Natanz plants and the deeply buried Fordow enrichment plant. It has stated plans to build a total of 10 enrichment plants and suspicions are growing that it is building another one in secret. It is operating a large power reactor at Bushehr and maintains relatively large uranium conversion and fuel fabrication facilities near Esfahan. It is nearing completion of a heavy water reactor at Arak that appears better suited to make plutonium for nuclear weapons than to produce medical isotopes for civilian use.

If Iran decided to produce nuclear explosive materials today, it could use its gas centrifuge program to produce weapon-grade uranium (WGU). However, Iran's fear of military strikes likely deters it at this time from producing WGU or nuclear weapons. However, if its centrifuge plants expand as currently planned, by the middle of 2014 these plants could have enough centrifuges to allow Iran to break out so quickly, namely rapidly produce WGU from its stocks of low enriched uranium, that the International Atomic Energy Agency (IAEA) would likely not detect this breakout until after Iran had produced enough WGU for one or two nuclear weapons. ISIS calls this a "critical capability."

If the Arak reactor operates, Iran could also create a plutonium pathway to nuclear weapons. This reactor can produce enough plutonium each year for one or two nuclear weapons, heightening concerns that Iran aims to build nuclear weapons. Its operation would needlessly complicate negotiations and increase the risk of military strikes.

CURRENT ENRICHMENT STATUS AND LOW ENRICHED URANIUM (LEU) STOCKS

Iran began enriching uranium in its main enrichment facility, the Fuel Enrichment Plant (FEP), near Natanz in February 2007. Over the past 6 years, Tehran has increased the number of enriching centrifuges at Natanz to more than 9,000 IR–1 centrifuges, added a set of tandem IR–1 centrifuge cascades in the Pilot Fuel Enrichment Plant (PFEP) at Natanz, and commenced enrichment at the fortified, underground Fordow Fuel Enrichment Plant (FFEP) in two sets of tandem IR–1 cascades. Additionally, Iran has worked to improve its cascade design and greatly increased its skill in operating centrifuge cascades. While the IR–1 is not an advanced centrifuge, and while its performance in Iran has been subpar, Iran's IR–1 cascades still could be employed effectively to make WGU.

Iran has in the last 2 years installed many thousands of additional centrifuges at its facilities. Although it has not begun enriching in these machines, the vast majority are fully installed and under vacuum, meaning that Iran could quickly begin feeding natural uranium into these cascades and more than double its enrichment capacity.

As of the August 2013 IAEA "Safeguards Report on Iran," Iran had installed an additional 6,250 IR–1 centrifuges for a total of 15,416 IR–1 centrifuges at the Natanz FEP. Iran has also begun installing its advanced centrifuge, the IR–2m, a centrifuge with a capacity three to five times greater than the IR–1 centrifuge, at the FEP. As of August, Iran had fully installed 1,008 IR–2m centrifuges there and was preparing to fully install over 3,000 of these machines at the FEP. Even if Iran installs no additional IR–2m centrifuges, these installed IR–2ms are equivalent to 3,000–5,000 IR–1 centrifuges.

Iran has nearly fully outfitted the Fordow facility with IR–1 centrifuges, although it continues to enrich in only 696 centrifuges. Another 2,014 IR–1 centrifuges are installed, for a total of 2,710 IR–1 centrifuges. If all these centrifuges are devoted to making near 20 percent LEU, Iran could nearly quadruple its output of this material to over 40 kilograms (kg) per month.

In total, at the Natanz pilot plant, the Natanz FEP, and the Fordow site, Iran has installed 18,454 IR–1 centrifuges in production-scale cascade. To this must be added the 1,008 IR-2m centrifuges installed at the FEP. These results are summarized in Table 1.

During this time, Iran has also enriched and stockpiled a significant amount of uranium. According to the August 2013 IAEA safeguards report, it has produced in total 9,704 kilograms of uranium hexafluoride enriched to 3.5 percent, some 2,877 kg of which has been further enriched at the Natanz pilot plant and the Fordow enrichment plant to produce 373 kg of near 20 percent LEU hexafluoride. As of August, Iran held a net 6,774 kg of 3.5 percent LEU hexafluoride and 186 kg of near 20 percent LEU hexafluoride, having converted a portion of its near 20 percent fuel to uranium oxide suitable for fuel assemblies for the Tehran Research Reactor (TRR). These stockpiles are monitored by the IAEA, but if Iran chose to break out from its obligations under the Nuclear Nonproliferation Treaty (NPT), the stored LEU in both hexafluoride and oxide form would be available for the production of WGU. Table 2 summarizes these inventories.

Based on the IAEA August 2013 safeguards report on Iran, Iran had converted no more than 30 kilograms of near 20 percent LEU, or 45 kilograms of near 20 percent LEU hexafluoride, into fuel assemblies for the TRR. This represents approximately 12 percent of Iran's total stock of near 20 percent enriched uranium, or only about 25 percent of the amount of LEU Iran has sent to Esfahan for conversion.

Unless the near 20 percent LEU oxide is converted to fuel assemblies and irradiated, it can relatively easily be reconverted to uranium hexafluoride suitable for further enrichment. Even if Iran began rapidly producing fuel assemblies for the TRR, due to the small size of the research reactor, Iran cannot realistically irradiate this fuel.

As such, conversion into an oxide form cannot be seen as a significant confidence-building measure on its own. Even so, Iran should be commended for taking measures to convert its uranium to uranium oxide at the Esfahan facility. Although conversion of uranium hexafluoride into uranium oxide and fabrication into fuel elements does limit Iran's ability to quickly use this material in a breakout scenario, the only iron-clad way to prevent its further enrichment is for an outside country to hold this material in escrow prior to irradiation.

Iran has been careful to convert sufficient near 20 percent LEU hexafluoride to keep its total stockpile of this material under the redline established by Israel of about 240–250 kilograms of near 20 percent LEU hexafluoride. These values are a rough measure of the amount of this LEU needed for further enrichment to produce about 25 kilograms of WGU, widely recognized as enough for a nuclear weapon.

These data show that Iran has produced far more LEU than it needs, whether the LEU is near 20 percent enriched or 3.5 percent enriched. Thus, a halt to enrichment would still leave Iran with a sizeable stock of LEU that is far in excess of its current needs.

IRAN'S SHORTENING BREAKOUT TIMES

A central consideration in assessing the threat of Iran building nuclear weapons is the timeline for Iran to acquire them following a decision to do so. The IAEA has concluded that Iran has the know-how to build a crude nuclear explosive device that it could detonate underground or deliver by aircraft or ship. It would take Iran longer to build a deliverable warhead for its Shahab 3 or Sajiil 2 ballistic missiles because Iran is believed to require more time to master the construction of a reliable, miniaturized warhead for these missiles.

Overall, Iran would likely need anywhere from a few months to about a year to build a crude nuclear explosive device and longer to build a warhead for a ballistic missile. The "long pole in the tent" of such an effort is Iran's lack of sufficient WGU. It is assessed as not possessing WGU, and thus its priority would be the production of enough for a nuclear weapon, or more likely several nuclear weapons.

In that light, Iran may seek to divert its existing stocks of LEU, enriching this material further up to weapon-grade as fast as it can. Iran's goal would be to accumulate enough weapon-grade uranium before it was detected and the United States and other nations responded, likely militarily destroying the facilities doing the enrichment.

Over the last several years, ISIS in collaboration with U.S. centrifuge specialists at the University of Virginia have estimated Iranian breakout times under a variety of circumstances. These estimates seek to determine a minimum time for Iran to accumulate enough weapon-grade uranium for a nuclear weapon. In practice, breakout times may be even longer than predicted. For example, Iran may know in theory how to enrich to weapon-grade but in practice may encounter difficulties and unexpected inefficiencies. Iran has found enrichment very difficult and far more time consuming than expected. Nonetheless, one central trend in these calculations is that as Iran has further developed its gas centrifuge capabilities and increased its inventories of LEU, breakout times have shortened significantly.

*How quickly could Iran break out today at the Natanz and Fordow enrichment plants?*

The two main enrichment sites at Natanz and Fordow contain a total of 18,454 IR–1 centrifuges (see Table 1). In order to conduct a dash using safeguarded LEU at Natanz and Fordow, Iran would need to violate its commitments under the NPT, including diverting the LEU from IAEA safeguards. In that effort, however, Iran would need to make only minor modifications in the enrichment plants before starting to enrich to weapon-grade levels. We assess that these modifications today would take at least 2 weeks to accomplish.

Recent estimates by the University of Virginia experts and ISIS incorporate the data from the August 2013 IAEA report on Iran. According to this estimate, if Iran used some of its existing stock of 3.5 percent LEU, all of its near 20 percent LEU hexafluoride, and all of its installed IR–1 centrifuges, it could dash to produce one significant quantity (SQ) of WGU needed for a nuclear weapon, or 25 kilograms of WGU, in 1.0–1.6 months. If it used in addition the installed IR-2m centrifuges at Natanz and Fordow, it could reduce this breakout time to 0.9–1.4 months.

If Iran chose to dash at these plants to WGU without using its near 20 percent LEU stockpile, it could produce 25 kg of WGU in 1.9–2.2 months with its IR–1 centrifuges, or in somewhat less time if it also used its installed IR-2m centrifuges at the FEP. Iran currently has enough 3.5 percent inventory to produce approximately 100 kg of WGU, according to this estimate.

These estimated breakout times today are sufficiently long enough to allow for detection by IAEA inspectors and a military response that could end further production. However, breakout times are growing dangerously short as Iran builds up its stock of near 20 percent LEU hexafluoride and installs more centrifuges.

### CRITICAL CAPABILITY

Although Iran is engaged in nuclear hedging, no evidence has emerged that the regime has decided to build nuclear weapons. Such a decision may be unlikely to occur until Iran is first able to augment its enrichment capability to a point where it would have the ability to make sufficient WGU quickly and secretly.

ISIS measures Iran's progress through an indicator called critical capability, shorthand for an Iranian capability to produce one or two weapons' worth of WGU using a stock of sufficient near 20 percent LEU while avoiding detection by the IAEA and time for action to be taken to stop it. Iran would achieve this capability principally by implementing its existing, firm plans to install thousands more IR–1 centrifuges, and perhaps a few thousand IR-2m centrifuges, at its declared Natanz and Fordow centrifuge sites and to learn to start up WGU production faster than it is judged capable of doing today. ISIS currently assesses that Iran will reach critical capability in mid-2014 if it continues on its current trajectory.

Iran's critical capability date could be achieved a few months earlier. For example, it could happen earlier if Iran successfully deployed and operated several thousand IR-2m centrifuges while continuing to install and operate more IR–1 centrifuges.

To delay this critical capability date, the most important condition that could be placed on Iran is achieving a halt to the installation of more centrifuges of any type. Any future nuclear agreement must include a limit on the number and type of centrifuges Iran can install. A numerical limit would need to be well below the number of centrifuges currently installed at Natanz and Fordow and below the number of centrifuges actually enriching in the summer of 2013, when the level was around 9,000 IR–1 centrifuges. In determining this limit, each IR-2m should be treated as equivalent to 3–5 IR–1 centrifuges. Once data are available on the ability of IR-2m cascades to enrich uranium, this equivalence can be better defined.

### NUCLEAR WEAPONS PROGRAM

During the last several weeks, Iranian officials, including President Hassan Rouhani and Foreign Minister Mohammad Javad Zarif have emphasized that Iran has never pursued or sought a nuclear bomb. Unfortunately, the available evidence provides little reason to believe them. If Iran wants the world to believe it will not build nuclear weapons in the future, the Iranian Government should reconsider its blanket denials of ever seeking nuclear weapons in the past.

The U.S. intelligence community in a "2007 National Intelligence Estimate" (NIE) stated: "We assess with high confidence that until fall 2003, Iranian military entities were working under government direction to develop nuclear weapons." It added: "We assess with moderate confidence Tehran had not restarted its nuclear weapons program as of mid-2007, but we do not know whether it currently intends to develop nuclear weapons." Our European allies, Britain, France, and Germany, agreed that Iran had a sizeable nuclear weapons program into 2003. However, they differed with the NIE's post-2003 conclusion. They assessed that Iran's nuclear weaponization program continued after 2003, albeit in a smaller and less structured manner.

A March 31, 2012 New York Times story by James Risen reported that the 2010 National Intelligence Estimate assessed that "while Iran had conducted some basic weapons-related research, it was not believed to have restarted the actual weapons program halted in 2003." In an earlier article on March 17, 2012, Risen wrote: "Iran says its nuclear program is for peaceful civilian purposes, but American intelligence agencies and the International Atomic Energy Agency have picked up evidence in recent years that some Iranian research activities that may be weapons-related have continued since 2003, officials said. That information has not been significant enough for the spy agencies to alter their view that the weapons program has not been restarted." But Risen reporting shows that U.S. intelligence found evidence that research on nuclear weapons may have continued after 2003.

These assessments are in line with the IAEA's findings. In its November 2011 safeguards report, the IAEA provided evidence of Iran's pre- and post-2003 nuclear weaponization efforts. The IAEA found, "The information indicates that prior to the end of 2003 [the activities] took place under a structured programme. There are also indications that some activities relevant to the development of a nuclear explosive device continued after 2003, and that some may still be ongoing." Several years of efforts by the IAEA to resolve these concerns have proven fruitless. The IAEA is scheduled to meet Iran in late October to discuss these issues again, where Iran has indicated it wants to make substantive progress.

Thus, these intelligence and IAEA assessments differ markedly with Iranian blanket denials about seeking nuclear weapons. Moreover, they share a view that Iran may have continued researching nuclear weapons in more recent times.

These intelligence agencies also share an assessment that Iran has not made a decision to build nuclear weapons. So, President Rouhani's pledge that Iran will not build nuclear weapons can still be realistic. And his apparent willingness to seek meaningful negotiations offers the first hope in several years that an agreement solving this nuclear crisis is possible. However, if Iran is unwilling to detail its past efforts to build nuclear weapons, or at the very least acknowledge the existence of a program, it undermines the credibility of statements about its present-day nuclear intentions.

If Iran truly does not intend to pursue nuclear weapons in the future, it should heed the experience of states that abandoned nuclear weapons. Brazil and South Africa described their past nuclear weapons efforts as part of their successful process to convince the international community that they had turned their back on nuclear weapons and would not seek them in the future. Brazil admitted its past nuclear weapons work at the start of its renunciations of all nuclear explosives. South Africa mistakenly chose the path of trying to deny that it ever had nuclear weapons as it limited its nuclear programs to civil activities and greatly increased transparency over its remaining nuclear programs. But South Africa's approach did not work; too many governments knew that it had had a nuclear weapons program and wondered if the deception meant that it was hiding ongoing nuclear weapons efforts. The IAEA, which was intensely investigating South Africa's nuclear activities, shared this skepticism. South Africa's deception poisoned the well.

In March 1993, President F.W. de Klerk announced to the world that indeed South Africa did have nuclear weapons but had destroyed them several years earlier. He invited the IAEA to verify his statements. The IAEA did so in a half year because of South Africa's remarkable cooperation with the inspectors. South Africa's pledge that it would never seek nuclear weapons again suddenly became much more credible. These transparency measures quickly convinced the world of South Africa's sincerity.

Iran may fear that it will be treated differently. The Iranian Government may reason that if it comes clean about its past activities, it will be punished by the international community. But other cases argue against such a response. The key is admitting these past activities should be part of a process of placing strategic limitations on its nuclear programs, instituting far greater transparency, and adhering to frankness about its past. The IAEA and governments can then develop confidence that Iran is not seeking nuclear weapons. But if Iran seeks to continue to hide its past military nuclear efforts, it may find that no amount of limitations and transparency on its current programs is enough to reassure the international community. Significant questions about its motives would most likely remain, and thus it would be less likely to gain the major relief from sanctions it so desperately seeks.

*Is Iran building a secret gas centrifuge plant?*

The question of whether Iran is building a third enrichment plant in secret has been an open one since then-Iranian nuclear chief, Ali Akbar Salehi, claimed on August 16, 2010, that "studies for the location of 10 other uranium enrichment facilities" had ended, and that "the construction of one of these facilities will begin by the end of the (current Iranian) year (March 2011) or start of the next year." Succeeding nuclear head, Fereydoun Abbasi-Davani, said in mid-2011 that construction on additional enrichment plants was delayed by 2 years. Now, over 2 years later, is Iran building a new centrifuge plant in addition to the Natanz and Fordow centrifuge plants? Or is the plant deferred for another year? Iran in the past secretly constructed the Natanz centrifuge site, the Kalaye Electric centrifuge research and development plant, and the deeply buried Fordow centrifuge facility.

Since March 2007, Iran has taken the position that it does not have to notify the IAEA if it begins construction of a nuclear facility, but the IAEA says that Iran has a legal obligation to do so under its current safeguards agreement. Iran's provision of information about the construction of any new enrichment sites is pertinent to instilling confidence about the peaceful nature of its nuclear activities and that it will not make weapon-grade uranium in secret.

It remains for Iran to abide by the simple provision of its IAEA safeguards agreement, modified Code 3.1, to provide the IAEA with advance information about its construction of additional enrichment facilities and to explain any current construction of a third enrichment site. In avoiding its responsibility under its safeguards agreement, Iran risks that any site subsequently discovered being built in secret will be viewed as a threat, increasing the risks of military confrontation and undermining the credibility of President Rouhani and the regime.

But an important question is how quickly could a secret site outfitted with IR-2m centrifuges produce WGU? Little is known about Iran's manufacture of these centrifuges or the total number manufactured to date or planned to be made in the next year. The IAEA is currently unable to monitor centrifuge manufacturing.

To understand this case better, ISIS and its University of Virginia collaborators performed two estimates. Each assumes that the covert plant contains 3,000 IR-2m centrifuges, a size consistent with the Fordow plant, and the plant design has other similarities to that of the Fordow plant (in particular that the covert plant is not optimized for weapon-grade uranium production). The output of each centrifuge is considered slightly more than about 3–5 times that of the IR–1 centrifuges.[1]

The first case considers that Iran would divert safeguarded stocks of LEU to this plant. The IAEA would detect the diversion of the LEU within a few weeks; however, the centrifuge site would be unknown and immune from military strikes, complicating enormously any U.S. or international response. In this case, Iran would use both of its 3.5-percent and near 20-percent LEU stocks, which are assumed to be at current levels. In this case, Iran could produce 25 kg of WGU in 1.3–2.3 months before using up its current stock of near 20 percent LEU stockpile. Without using its 20-percent stockpile, and using only its 3.5-percent LEU stock, Iran could produce 25 kg of WGU in 2.2–4.5 months with enough 3.5 percent inventory for approximately 100 WGU. If Iran had sufficient near 20 percent LEU for one nuclear weapon, it could reduce breakout times to about 1 month.

The second case is that Iran would not use its safeguarded LEU but a secret stock of natural uranium hexafluoride that it produced at a secret production plant. In this case, Iran would need 6.4 to 11 months to produce 25 kg of WGU.

IDENTIFYING AND ASSESSING NECESSARY CONCESSIONS BY IRAN IN NEGOTIATIONS

As part of understanding the proposed negotiating process, it is useful to discuss the range of concessions that Iran could make in order to gain confidence that it is not seeking nuclear weapons. Incentives involving sanctions relief are equally important and are not considered here but an ISIS report prepared for the U.S. Institute of Peace includes this analysis. The following list includes a wide range

---

[1] Each IR-2m centrifuge is assumed to have an output of 3–5 separative work units per year.

of Iranian concessions. The final list would of course be decided in a negotiation and Iran may or may not agree to all of the following:

*Resolving outstanding issues with the IAEA over the military dimension*

- Address cooperatively the IAEA's concerns over its past and possibly ongoing military nuclear activities. "Coming clean," or detailing past work on nuclear weapons, remains critical.

*Limiting breakout times*

- End production of any more near 20 percent LEU and commit not to enrich uranium over 5 percent. Dismantle and decommission the tandem cascades at the Fordow site and the Natanz Pilot Fuel Enrichment plant.
- Send out under IAEA custody stocks of near 20 percent LEU in excess of near-term needs of the Tehran Research Reactor.
- Decommission the Fordow enrichment site.
- Commit not to assemble a production line to reconvert enriched $U_3O_8$ to UF6, whatever its enrichment level.
- Freeze the number and type of Iran's installed centrifuges to below an equivalent of 10,000 IR–1 centrifuges. Limit enrichment to the Natanz site only.
- Send out under IAEA custody excess stocks of LEU enriched below 5 percent. Stocks could be considered excess if over the next several years, they are unlikely to be used to fuel a nuclear reactor. The total stock should be less than the equivalent of 1 tonne of LEU hexafluoride.
- Convert all LEU remaining in Iran first into an oxide form and then into a solid fuel form.
- Halt production of LEU enriched less than 5 percent, unless there is an economic need for domestically produced LEU fuel in a reactor.
- Halt the construction of centrifuge components and the assembly of centrifuges, except a limited number to replace broken centrifuges at existing enrichment sites.

*Increasing transparency*

- Enhance IAEA monitoring, including:
    - Æ Implementing early notification of the construction of nuclear plants (or more formally implement modified code 3.1. of the Subsidiary Arrangements to Iran's Comprehensive Safeguards Agreement);
    - Æ Ratifying the Additional Protocol;
    - Æ Increasing the monitoring of centrifuge production and assembly facilities; and
    - Æ Establishing remote monitoring at key nuclear sites.

*Ending a plutonium pathway*

- Halt the construction and operation of the Arak heavy water reactor. Initiate studies to determine the feasibility and cost of converting the reactor to a light water moderator and LEU fuel.
- Commit not to conduct any plutonium separation or reprocessing activities.

*Halting illicit nuclear trade and proliferation to other countries*

- Commit not to engage in nuclear smuggling to obtain any goods for its nuclear or missile programs. Key nuclear- and missile-related sanctions would become verification mechanisms to ensure Iran's compliance with its agreements.
- Agree not to proliferate nuclear technologies to other countries.

Experts may differ over the relative importance of each concession, and negotiators may add or subtract concessions. However, most of these concessions would be expected to be needed in a final agreement that would establish confidence that Iran is not seeking nuclear weapons and that would provide confidence that an Iranian effort to do so would be detected in a timely manner, allowing adequate time for an international response to prevent Iran from successfully building nuclear weapons. As such, this list of concessions provides an indication of the difficult work needed to achieve an agreement that would lead to a significant reduction of sanctions.

Some would argue that all of these concessions are not possible to achieve in an agreement with Iran. In that case, it is important to consider tradeoffs. Some can undoubtedly be weakened or avoided. Whether the agreement allows 5,000 or 10,000 IR–1 centrifuges may not matter that much if other conditions are in place. Likewise, the tonnage of 3.5 percent LEU in Iran is certainly adjustable. Perhaps no 3.5 percent LEU needs to leave Iran. Some may also be startled by a condition to make the enrichment of LEU dependent on an economic evaluation of the need for reactor fuel, but such a condition is what drives most civilian nuclear programs. And if there is a settlement, Iran would be able to buy reactor fuel abroad at a lower cost than required to make the fuel itself. The imported fuel would be safer and more reliable, given that it would come from venders with decades of experience. Thus, an economic constraint on the enrichment of uranium is reasonable and would certainly make verification of any agreement easier.

In some cases, dropping a concession could be highly problematic for the success of an agreement. For example, it is instructive to consider that Iran is now sticking by its story that it never had a nuclear weapons program and this would not satisfy the IAEA in its investigation about past and possibly ongoing nuclear weapons work. In this case, there would remain significant suspicions about whether Iran is maintaining a capability to build nuclear weapons. In response, an agreement would probably need to contain much more stringent limitations on Iran's enrichment capabilities and its centrifuge manufacturing facilities. Likely, many would demand that Iran agree to zero centrifuges or the dismantlement of its centrifuge program, a condition not included above, or a cap of far fewer centrifuges than the equivalent of 10,000 IR–1 centrifuges mentioned above. These concerns are driven by numerous verification uncertainties generated by an active, relatively large centrifuge program, and the IAEA currently having little hope of finding secret nuclear sites or verifying their absence. Iran's ratification of the Additional Protocol would help but even that may not be sufficient for the IAEA to determine with high enough confidence the absence of a secret centrifuge site to satisfy key IAEA member states, particularly when ambiguities arise, as is inevitable in such a complicated agreement. Moreover, under an Additional Protocol, or even the current Comprehensive Safeguards Agreement, the inspectors would be obligated to return over and over again to these alleged nuclear weapons issues as part of determining on an ongoing basis the correctness and completeness of Iran's nuclear declaration and developing confidence that no nuclear material has been diverted to a nuclear weapons program. The main difference would be that the Additional Protocol would grant the IAEA more tools to pursue their completeness investigations, generating more opportunities for conflict between Iran and the IAEA. Instructing the IAEA not to determine the completeness of Iran's declaration could damage the IAEA's credibility and greatly undermine confidence in ability to verify an agreement.

Thus, some concessions may be obligatory if an agreement is to succeed. It is imperative to determine the critical concessions and the risks posed by omitting others as soon as possible.

ADDITIONAL MEASURES TO LIMIT IRAN'S ABILITY TO EXPAND ITS NUCLEAR PROGRAMS

The chairman has also asked for additional measures to pressure Iran and limit its ability to outfit its nuclear programs. ISIS just released a major report, the "Future World of Illicit Nuclear Trade: Mitigating the Threat," written in part under a grant from the Project on Advanced Systems and Concepts for Countering Weapons of Mass Destruction (PASCC) at the Center on Contemporary Conflict, Naval Postgraduate School. This report is the result of a 2-year original research effort and contains a characterization of future threats over the next 5 to 10 years related to augmented nuclear trafficking worldwide and more than 100 recommendations aimed at preventing the emergence of these threats, including many related to better limiting Iran's nuclear progress.

I would like to mention two key recommendations detailed in our report that would increase the effectiveness of sanctions against Iran's nuclear programs. They are:

- The U.S. Government would announce it will designate China and Hong Kong, key persistent trans-shippers of U.S. goods to Iran's nuclear program despite years of diplomatic overtures, as destinations of diversion concern under the Comprehensive Iran Sanctions, Accountability, and Divestment Act (CISADA) unless they make concrete changes within a given grace period. Just the threat of making this designation could inspire action on the parts of China and Hong Kong, as it did with the United Arab Emirates in 2007. If made official, such designations could reduce the supply to Iran of proliferation-sensitive goods, services, or technologies by: enhancing scrutiny by U.S. Government licensing agencies of specific proliferation-sensitive exports from the United States to China and Hong Kong; increasing pressure on the Chinese and Hong Kong authorities to crack down on diversion through their territories to Iranian end-users and Iranian intermediaries; and helping secure support from other countries which likewise face challenges in ensuring that sales to China and Hong Kong do not end up in Iran, allowing it to expand its nuclear programs.
- The U.S. Government should increase its use of sting operations and investigations aimed at stopping Iran's illicit nuclear procurement networks and launch

a major effort to encourage other governments to initiate their own sting operations against trafficking in nuclear-related commodities. Few governments conduct this type of sting operation, and U.S. sting operations against Iranian smugglers have been particularly effective. Implementing this recommendation would help create an additional risk factor for Iran and those helping Iran outfit its nuclear programs. The United States should work with global partners to assist them and coordinate with them on conducting their own or joint sting operations.

TABLE 1.—NUMBER OF CENTRIFUGES ENRICHING AND/OR INSTALLED IN IRAN

| LOCATION | IR-1 Centrifuges enriching | IR-1 Centrifuges installed * | IR-2m Centrifuges enriching | IR-2m Centrifuges installed |
|---|---|---|---|---|
| FEP | 9,166 | 15,416 | 0 | 1,008 |
| PFEP** | 328 | 328 | 0** | N/A |
| FFEP | 696 | 2,710 | 0 | 0 |
| Total | 10,190 | 18,454 | 0 | 1,008 |

* Number of centrifuges installed includes enriching centrifuges.
** Iran has installed a number of different types of centrifuge in different cascade configurations at the PFEP. This table disregards centrifuges from which Iran recombines product and tails.

TABLE 2.—CUMULATIVE TOTALS OF NATURAL AND ENRICHED URANIUM FEED AND 3.5 AND 19.75 PERCENT LEU HEXAFLUORIDE PRODUCT IN IRAN

| LOCATION | 0.711 percent feed | 3.5 percent LEU product | 3.5 percent LEU feed | 19.75 percent LEU product |
|---|---|---|---|---|
| FEP | 110,590 kg | 9,704 kg | N/A | N/A |
| PFEP | N/A | N/A | 1,455 kg | 178 kg |
| FFEP | N/A | N/A | 1,422 kg | 195 kg |
| Gross Total | 110,590 kg | 9,704 kg | 2,877 kg | 373 kg |
| Net Total | 110,590 kg | 6,774 kg* | 2,877 kg | 186 kg** |

* Number is less 3.5 percent enriched uranium hexafluoride used as feedstock at the PFEP and FFEP as well as 53 kg 3.5 percent LEU hexafluoride converted to uranium oxide.
** Number is less 185 kg of 19.75 percent LEU hexafluoride fed into the process at the Esfahan conversion and fuel fabrication plants and 1.6 kg 19.75 percent LEU hexafluoride down blended.

The CHAIRMAN. Ambassador Jeffrey.

## STATEMENT OF HON. JAMES F. JEFFREY, PHILIP SOLONDZ DISTINGUISHED VISITING FELLOW, THE WASHINGTON INSTITUTE FOR NEAR EAST POLICY, WASHINGTON, DC

Ambassador JEFFREY. Thank you very much, Mr. Chairman, Mr. Ranking Member, for inviting me here today.

First of all, I agree with what Dr. Albright has said, and that will shorten my comments considerably.

We do have an opportunity through this latest set of actions associated with Mr. Rouhani to perhaps find a negotiated outcome. There is a possibility that we will avert either a military action and possibly war or, what would be even worse, a nuclear-armed, a nuclear-capable Iran.

The devil is going to be in the details. There have been various attempts to achieve a breakthrough. At one point in 2009, the Iranians accepted a very broad limitation on their enrichment, either moving out enriched uranium, or limiting what they would do, but then they reneged on it. Then, in 2010, under different circumstances, they accepted a somewhat different plan.

So there is some room for maneuver in here, but the details are going to be very, very difficult, involving the sequencing of sanctions, which sanctions to withdraw. The question of enrichment, whether at all? If so, under what conditions? How much?

You discussed this in very considerable detail with Secretary Sherman, and she was, as expected, very general on where the administration was on this because this is going to be basically much of the core of the negotiations. But what I would like to do is very quickly give a couple of more broad contextual aspects of this.

First of all, the reason that we are so concerned about this nuclear weapon potential, compared to a nuclear-armed neighbor of Iran's—Pakistan, or even North Korea, and I think here that Secretary Sherman's comment that Iran is sui generis is correct—is because Iran is a different kind of animal. It has a regional claim to power that goes deep into the population, deep into its history. It presents the kind of problem we had with Milosevic a decade plus ago, the kind of problem we had with Saddam Hussein.

The Iranians are going to be very unlikely to give up this regional quest for power, for hegemony, and the various tools, nuclear, terrorism, alliances with Syria, Hezbollah, and on and on. We can get them to push back on one or another thing when we put enough pressure on them, such as the nuclear issue. But this is a long-term conflict we are in with Iran. Even if we do get a breakthrough on the nuclear account, we are not going to resolve the conflict and we should bear that in mind.

The second thing is what we have that has brought us to this point is very successful synergy between military threats, and the sanctions regime that Wendy Sherman went through the statistics on. They have been verified publicly. It is a very dramatic drop in oil, almost 60 percent of their exports have been cut.

And thirdly, the cooperation of the international community because it is mainly the international community that has to carry out these sanctions at the price of being denied access to the U.S. banking system. So these three elements are very important to keep in balance.

I am very concerned about the credibility of the U.S. military threat. The President took a step in the right direction the other day with Prime Minister Netanyahu, when he named specifically—among the ''all options are on the table, nothing is off''—he named specifically military force.

That is important. We have to keep emphasizing that. Because what I am hearing in the region, I have been out there, is that people are doubting us. And it is very important that this military credibility remain intact.

On the other hand, we have to be very watchful of our allies and our friends in the P5+1 and the people who are carrying out the sanctions because we need to have as much international cooperation as possible, both to get a deal, to continue to put pressure on Iranians, and, if necessary if we have to go to military action, to support us there.

I will stop there.

[The prepared statement of Ambassador Jeffrey follows:]

PREPARED STATEMENT OF AMBASSADOR JAMES F. JEFFREY

Mr. Chairman, Mr. Ranking Member, Senators, thank you for the opportunity to appear before your committee on this critical matter.

The rapid pace of events since IranianPpresident Hassan Rouhani took office this past summer has significantly increased the possibility of a successful negotiation on Iran's nuclear program, thereby forestalling either a military strike on Iran or the emergence of a nuclear-armed or nuclear-weapon-capable Iran. Either of these latter eventualities would unleash unknown but likely very serious consequences on an already stressed international situation. The United States thus should vigorously engage, with Iran and with our allies and partners, accepting risks when necessary, to achieve a diplomatic breakthrough that would meet President Obama's criteria of being meaningful, transparent, and verifiable.

The technical outlines of any such agreement have been sketched out many times, by the P5+1 in its September 2009 offer to Iran and in studies and essays by many analysts, myself included. Iran will have to largely forgo use of its huge enrichment infrastructure, including closing the Fordow site, stop work on the Arak heavy water reactor, agree to much more intrusive IAEA inspections and implementation of a safeguards agreement, and come clean on its nuclear-related military research. Iran will insist on enrichment as a principle, but that would have to be limited in quantity and quality—that is, no more than 5 percent, with all but immediately required enriched uranium stored "temporarily" outside Iran and the whole process vigorously monitored. The P5+1 will have to lift or suspend nonmilitary sanctions, especially those targeting hydrocarbons trade and banking not tied to illicit nuclear materials trade, and de facto will have to countenance a minimal amount of Iranian enrichment.

While the outline of such a "big for big" deal can be sketched out as above, two sets of detail-related issues will be-devil the negotiations. The first is operational: how to sequence tit-for-tat concessions and intermediary steps to move toward "big for big" in a low-trust environment. The second involves the two core concessions: enrichment and sanctions relief. The Iranians have repeatedly demanded formal international recognition of a "right to enrichment." The P5+1 should resist this demand. The right to enrichment is informally anchored in the Nuclear Nonproliferation Treaty, and has been explicitly annulled by legally binding U.N. Security Council resolutions. The most the P5+1 should do is void or, better, suspend the ban on enrichment as a "quid" for Iranian accommodation.

The sanctions relief problem cuts two ways: first, difficulty reinstating international sanctions once lifted or canceled, given their economic disadvantages and possible noncooperation by Russia and China, thereby undercutting the "stick" component of any deal; and, second, likely reluctance by many in Congress to lift sanctions for any inevitably less-than-perfect agreement, thus undercutting the "carrot" needed for any deal.

A solution to the two-headed sanctions problem could focus on temporary "test" arrangements. U.N. and EU sanctions could be suspended for X period, following which they would automatically kick back in, absent new votes to extend or make permanent the sanctions relief, based on the degree of verified Iranian compliance. On the key U.S. sanctions—namely, the highly effective 2012 National Defense Authorization Act, which imposed bank penalties for funding Iranian oil purchases—the President in consultation with Congress could exercise the national security waiver in the act. To avoid a strong congressional reaction, any agreement would have to be at least minimally acceptable to Israel and a majority in Congress. Iran in turn would have to accept, at least initially, temporary, contingent sanctions relief in return for its concessions and actions (which themselves would be reversible).

But even if these tough issues could be resolved, the opportunity to reach agreement remains only a possibility. To increase the chances of it becoming a reality, the following should be kept in mind in executing our diplomatic strategy.

First, Iran's foreign policy reflects long-term regional ambitions amounting to de facto hegemony, broadly supported by the population. With or without an agreement, with or without more mutual trust with the outside world, these ambitions are unlikely to change, and they are inimical to the interests of the other states in the region, to the United States and its world role, and to an international community based on the U.N. charter. But we should neither demand that Iran give up these ambitions as the condition for any agreement, nor "sell" any agreement as a gateway to a friendlier Iran. Any agreement must rest on its own merits as a better alternative to military action or a nuclear Iran. Any acceptable agreement would perhaps improve understanding and trust between Iran and the outside world. While this would be a good thing for crisis management between hostile camps, it should not be an expectation from, or motivation for, doing a deal. Given this underlying reality, the United States should absolutely avoid concessions in return for "enhanced trust" or "good chemistry."

Second, we are at this hopeful point only because of the threat of U.S. or Israeli military action, the impact of U.N., EU, and especially U.S. sanctions on the Iranian economy, population, and political system, and the willingness of the international community to accept these sanctions despite their costs. Thus, nothing done inside or outside the negotiations should weaken these three pillars and their necessary synergy.

Third, it would be a mistake in any negotiation to hold international sanctions relief and other benefits hostage to a change in Iran's fundamental worldview and ambitions, or abandonment of its specific activities beyond the nuclear account, from internal oppression and support of terror to engagement in Syria. Iran's nuclear effort is a tactical sortie that in the face of sufficient pressure can be at least temporarily abandoned. Iran, however, is highly unlikely to yield to pressure on its fundamental interests, as it sees them. And any effort to compel it to do so will likely strengthen those who argue that a nuclear agreement is really a Trojan horse for regime change. Pushing such an agenda would not only scuttle negotiations but likely mobilize in opposition to the United States much of the international community needed for continued U.S. sanctions. As Congress considers new sanctions, it will be important to consider the timeline for their implementation.

Finally, the credible threat of military force must overshadow any negotiating effort; not so obvious as to be provocative but present enough to be credible. Here, American will to act is as critical as American military capabilities. Frankly, the administration, beginning with its Afghanistan and Libya decisions and on to the President's May terrorism speech and punt to Congress on the Syria strike, has called our will into question. This can be reversed by our military readiness, more clarity on the administration's redline, a Presidential commitment to act on his own authority if the line is crossed, and expressions of congressional support for such action. However, the credibility of any threat of military force and other sticks is also enhanced if the United States puts a reasonable and comprehensive offer on the table. As seen in the runups to U.S. strikes in 1991, 2001, and 2003, the international community's vital support for military action is only attainable if the United States demonstrates it has taken every effort to offer a fair compromise.

Pulling off a diplomatic coup of the present magnitude will require extraordinary effort, as the administration must deal simultaneously with the Iranians, our European allies, Russia and China, an Israel and Arab Gulf deeply skeptical of any compromise with Iran, an American public generally opposed to the use of force, and a Congress sharing seemingly the attitudes of both the American people and the regional skeptics. But the current standoff between Iran and the rest of the world is inherently unstable, and the alternatives apart from a negotiated settlement—a nuclear-armed or capable Iran, or a new war—in the midst of a region already slipping out of control, are far worse.

The CHAIRMAN. Thank you, Ambassador.
Mr. Takeyh.

## STATEMENT OF RAY TAKEYH, SENIOR FELLOW FOR MIDDLE EASTERN STUDIES, COUNCIL ON FOREIGN RELATIONS, WASHINGTON, DC

Dr. TAKEYH. Thank you very much, Mr. Chairman, Senator Corker, for inviting me, and it is a great pleasure again for me to be here with Ambassador Jeffrey and my old friend, David Albright.

I think the Presidency of Hassan Rouhani has been greeted with assertions ranging from cautious optimism to euphoric anticipations of rapprochement. President Rouhani has been described in various ways as a reformer, a pragmatist, by his critics as a wolf in sheep's clothing.

Although it is often suggested that President Rouhani is under significant domestic pressure at home, I think those claims are grossly exaggerated, if not overstated. The Islamic Republic has established a consensus on its core security issues, including the nuclear issue. That consensus may prove fragile and may be subject to internal censure. But the notion that he is under political pressure and, therefore, requires international assistance is, I think, overstated.

Despite the softened rhetoric, we can count on the new Iranian regime to continue to assert as what it regards as its nuclear rights and press its advantages in a contested Middle East. The Islamic Republic will remain an important backer of the Assad dynasty, a benefactor of Hezbollah, a supporter of Palestinian rejectionist groups. It will persist its repressive tactics at home and deny fundamental human rights to its population. It is a government that will seek a negotiated settlement to the nuclear issue, but on terms that it will find advantageous.

Hassan Rouhani's case is not without its contradictions. He insists that Iran can expand its nuclear program while reclaiming its commercial contracts, even though the program today stands in violation of security council resolution tone and style matter. But what should await President Rouhani is a hard tradeoff dispensing with critical aspects of the program in exchange for  sanctions relief.

It needs to be stressed that the United States is entering these negotiations with important advantages. Iran's economy is faltering. Its population is disaffected. It is distrusted by its neighbors. This is a time for Washington to negotiate a maximalist agreement and not settle for Iranian half measures and half steps.

Although much of the attention recently, for obvious reasons, has been focused on the President Rouhani and his Foreign Minister, Javad Zarif, certainly an urbane and intelligent man, I want to draw attention on the Supreme National Security Council, which will actually make the fundamental nuclear decisions.

The nuclear file has not been transferred to the foreign ministry. The negotiations and representation of the nuclear file has been transferred to the foreign ministry. The Supreme National Security Council has also had new staff members. Their names are not in the press, and they do not give interviews.

It is headed today by Adm. Ali Shamkhani, a founding member of the Revolutionary Guards and an official long involved in Iran's nuclear program. He has recently appointed as his deputy a shadowy Revolutionary Guard figure, Ali Hosseini-Tash, who has been involved in the Iranian program from the very beginning.

As Ambassador Jeffrey has suggested, their vision of Iran is one of a hegemonic Iran, a strong Iran, a preeminent, if not a pivotal power in the region. Their newly empowered leadership  at  the helm at the Supreme National Security Council also has been very much committed to their nuclear capability and has been involved in procurement efforts.

Hosseini-Tash in one interview said, ''The nuclear program is an opportunity for us to make endeavors to acquire a strategic position and consolidate our national identity.''

They believe in a measure of restraint. As Iran presses its nuclear strategy, they recognize the importance of offering some confidence-building measures to a skeptical international community. All this is not to suggest that Iran is inclined to suspend its program, relinquish its critical components. But as I mentioned, they may be open to dialogue.

And they stress the Iranian reasonableness, the idea is that if Iran presents itself as a more reasonable actor, then its nuclear program can be sanctioned. Not sanctioned the way you are thinking of it—accepted, acknowledged.

Hovering over all of this is Supreme Leader Ali Khamenei. His instincts are to call for defiance in pursuit of the bomb. In his role as guardian of the state, of course, he must consider their nuclear program in context of Iran's larger concerns.

In recent months, he has opted for a strategy that takes into account his competing mandates. On the one hand, he presses for expansion of the nuclear program. On the other hand, he has accepted the need for negotiations and perhaps a measure of restraint.

Khamenei hopes that his new President can somehow square the many circles that confront him and somehow make the Iranian program more acceptable to the international community. So as we go forward, we have to be cautious about some of the changes that are taking place.

Thank you, Mr. Chairman.

[The prepared statement of Dr. Takeyh follows:]

PREPARED STATEMENT OF DR. RAY TAKEYH

THE ROUHANI PRESIDENCY: A KINDER, GENTLER ISLAMIC REPUBLIC?

The Presidency of Hassan Rouhani has been greeted with assertions ranging from cautious optimism to euphoric anticipations of an unfolding rapprochement. President Rouhani has been at times described as a reformer, a pragmatist, and by his critics as a "wolf in sheep's clothing." Although it is often suggested that President Rouhani is under significant pressure from hard-line elements at home, the Islamic Republic appears to have established a consensus on its core security concerns. That consensus may prove fragile, and subject to internal censure, but the notion that Rouhani is under political stress is overstated.

Despite its soften rhetoric, we can count on the new Iranian regime to continue asserting its nuclear "rights" and press its advantages in a contested Middle East. The Islamic Republic will remain an important backer of the Assad dynasty, a benefactor of Hezbollah, and a supporter of Palestinian rejectionist groups. It will persist with its repressive tactics and deny its populace their fundamental human rights. It is also a government that will seek a negotiated settlement on the nuclear issue and will strive to test the limits of the great powers' prohibitions.

*Who is Hassan Rouhani?*

Hassan Rouhani is a long-time regime insider with a deep commitment to the Islamic Republic and its nuclear aspirations. Unlike many of the Iran's previous leaders, it is possible to develop an understanding of Rouhani's thinking through his own published books, most notably his account of his time as Iran's chief nuclear negotiator.

Historians often suggest that Iran's clerical regime resurrected the Shah's atomic infrastructure after Iraq invaded the country in 1980. In this telling, deterrence and self-reliance are at the core of Iranian nuclear calculus. But Rouhani says the revolutionaries' attraction to nuclear science actually began when they were still lingering in exile. In 1979, when Ayatollah Ruhollah Khomeini and his disciples appeared certain to assume power, an Iranian scientific delegation journeyed to Paris and implored the aging mullah to scrap the nuclear program, which was exorbitant and inefficient. The cagy Khomeini ignored such pleas. A year before Saddam Hussein's armies attacked Iran, Khomeini had decided to preserve his nuclear inheritance.

During the initial decade of the Islamic Republic, the regime's preoccupation with consolidating power and prosecuting its war with Iraq eclipsed other priorities. Still, Rouhani describes a determined effort to secure nuclear technologies from abroad and complete the fuel cycle—an essential precursor to development of nuclear arms. Those efforts were redoubled during Ali Akbar Rafsanjani's Presidency in the early

1990s and were sustained by the reformist President Muhammad Khatami. Indeed, Rouhani is at pains to disentangle nuclear policy from Iran's contentious politics, insisting that all governments share credit for the program's progress.

Rouhani spent much of his tenure negotiating with the European powers—Britain, France and Germany—over what kind of nuclear program Iran was allowed to have. The signature event of his time as a negotiator was his country's voluntary suspension of its program in 2004. Those were heady days in the Middle East, with America's shock-and-awe campaign in Iraq intimidating other recalcitrant regimes, such as Iran, into accommodation. "No one thought that Saddam's regime would fall in 3 weeks," Rouhani recalls. "The military leadership had anticipated that Saddam would not fall easily and that America would have to fight the Iraqi army for at least 6 months to a year before reaching Saddam's palace." Yet, the proximity of American guns behooved the theocracy to act with caution.

Whatever political backing Rouhani has among Iran's reformers, he is not one of them; political freedom has rarely been a priority for him. During the late 1990s, when Khatami and his allies were seeking to expand individual rights and strengthen Iran's anemic civil society, Rouhani was indifferent to their efforts. Still, unlike his militant predecessor, he belongs to the more tempered wing of the theocracy that sees the nuclear debate in a larger context of Iran's international relations. In the recent Presidential race, Rouhani stressed the importance of the economy—in particular Iran's declining standard of living.

Rouhani's case is not without its contradictions. He insists that Iran can expand its nuclear program while reclaiming its commercial contracts, even though today Iran stands in violation of numerous U.N. Security Council resolutions and cannot reenter the global economy until it meets U.N. demands. Tone and style matter, but what awaits President Rouhani is the hard tradeoff of dispensing with critical aspects of the program in exchange for relief from sanctions. It needs to be stressed that the United States is entering these negotiations with important advantages. Iran's economy is railing and its population is disaffected. This is a time for Washington to negotiate a maximalist deal and not settled for Iranian half-measures and half-steps.

*Who is in charge?*

Although much of the focus since the Iranian Presidential election has been on Rouhani and his thoughtful and urbane Foreign Minister Muhammad Javad Zarif, the critical decisions will be made in the Supreme National Security Council (SNSC). The composition of that body and its newly installed leadership tells us more about the direction that Iran is going to take then Rouhani and Zarif's speeches, press briefings, and tweets.

The SNSC is increasingly being populated by a cohort of conservatives who spent much of their careers in the security services and the military. The head of the SNSC today is Ali Shamkhani, a founding member of the Revolutionary Guards and an official long involved in Iran's nuclear procurement efforts. Shamkhani has chosen as his deputy a shadowy Revolutionary Guard officer, Ali Husseini-Tash, who has long been involved in Iran's nuclear deliberations. The essence of these new leaders worldview is that since September 2001, Iran has a unique opportunity to emerge as the preeminent state of the region. However, over the past 8 years, Mahmoud Ahmadinejad's unwise provocations and his unnecessarily hostile rhetoric has paradoxically thwarted those ambitions. They argue that the only way for the Islamic Republic to reach its desired status is to present itself as a more reasonable actor while increasing its power. Such an Iran would have to impose some limits on the expressions of its influence, accede to certain global norms, and be prepared to negotiate mutually acceptable compacts with its adversaries.

It is important to stress that despite their interest in diplomacy and embrace of a more tempered language, the new cast of characters in charge of the SNSC perceive that Iran must claim its hegemonic role. Given the displacement of Iran's historic enemies in Afghanistan and Iraq, they sense that it is a propitious time for the Islamic Republic to claim the mantle of regional leadership. Iran has finally been offered a rare historical opportunity to emerge as the predominant power of the Persian Gulf region and a pivotal state in the Middle East. Whether they are correct in their assessments of regional trends, the salient point is that such perceptions condition their approach to international politics.

The newly empowered conservatives at the helm also believe that to enhance its influence Iran needs a nuclear capability. As the newly appointed deputy head of the SNSC, Husseini-Tash once noted, "The nuclear program is an opportunity for us to make endeavors to acquire a strategic position and consolidate our national identity." But they also believe in a measure of restraint. As Iran plots its nuclear strategy, they recognize the importance of offering confidence-building measures to a skeptical international community. All this is not to suggest that Iran is inclined to suspend the program or relinquish its critical components, but they are more open to dialogue. Moreover, they stress that a reasonable Iran can assuage U.S. concerns about its nuclear development without having to abandon the program.

At the core, all disarmament agreements call upon a state to forgo a certain degree of sovereignty in exchange for enhanced security. Once a state renounces its weapons of mass destruction program it can be assured of support from the international community should it be threatened by another state possessing such arms. This implied tradeoff has no value for Iran's rulers. The prolonged war with Iraq conditions their worldview and behavior. Iraq's use of chemical weapons against Iran has reinforced Iran's suspicions of the international community. For many of the Islamic Republic's leaders, the only way to safeguard Iran's interests is to develop an independent nuclear deterrent.

Hovering over all this is Iran's Supreme Leader Ali Khamenei. The Supreme Leader's instincts would be to support the reactionary elements in their call for defiance and pursuit of the bomb. But in his role as the guardian of state, he must consider the nuclear program in the context of Iran's larger concerns. In the recent months, he has opted for an approach that takes into account his competing mandates. On the one hand, he has pressed for acceleration of Iran's program and construction of an advanced nuclear infrastructure. Yet, he has also conceded the need for negotiations and pressed the state toward a degree of restraint. Khamenei hopes that his new President can somehow square the many circles that confront him, and somehow make the Iranian nuclear program more acceptable to the international community. He will be cautiously assessing Rouhani's diplomacy, ready to impose the necessary restrains should the new team be prone to compromise Iran's core concerns.

In assessing a state's nuclear path, it is important to note that its motivations cannot be exclusively examined within the context of its national interests and security considerations. Whatever strategic benefits such weapons offer a state, they are certainly a source of national prestige and parochial benefits to various bureaucracies and politicians. As such constituencies emerge, a state can cross the nuclear threshold even if the initial strategic factors that provoked the program are no longer salient. The emergence of bureaucracies can generate its own proliferation momentum, empowering those seeking a nuclear breakout. As time passes, the pragmatic voices calling for hedging are likely to be marginalized and lose their influence within the regime.

The CHAIRMAN. Thank you all for your testimony.

And Mr. Takeyh, I want to take off where you just finished. Is it that the Iranians have come to a conclusion domestically, maybe because of the sanctions, maybe because of other events, that they will have to, in essence, dramatically change their nuclear program? Or is it that they want to see if they can preserve the greatest amount of their nuclear program but relieve the sanctions?

Dr. TAKEYH. I think it is the latter. I think the intent is to preserve the program, at least what is there, the infrastructure that has already been created, the plutonium route, the two enrichment facilities, as well as the introduction of new generation of centrifuges which can operate with efficiency at high velocity.

I think the intention is to preserve all that, but perhaps as an interim measure, negotiate over expansion of the program in exchange for sanctions relief. And they are not talking about waivers. They are talking about fundamental sanctions relief.

The CHAIRMAN. And let me turn to you, Dr. Albright. What is the consequence of that? If we accept that, what is the consequence? What is the risk?

I have the concern that we create sanctions relief for less than what the Security Council has established, which means the world, not just the United States. The world has established through four Security Council resolutions what it believes is the standard of what Iran needs to do. And if you accept less, do you run the risk that you are in a position in which Iran, if it changes the course of events after all of these agreements are had, a year or two from now, that we are largely back to where we are at?

Dr. ALBRIGHT. Certainly, excuse me, the risk is that they would continue developing this capability, and it would, in essence, reduce breakout times, perhaps give a greater capability to build covert centrifuge plants. And so, I think the Iranian goal is probably not much different than it was in 2005 when the negotiations broke down is, they are willing to pause, but they are not willing to commit not to grow their centrifuge program.

And that was an essential roadblock back then was it is not good enough that they for a couple years do not make it—do not install more centrifuges, a few transparency measures, and then after those few years, they will just grow again. And then maybe they will pause again. But it is still their proposals have tended to be that the program will grow, and they will not shrink it.

And I think that this test is going to be very hard for Iran to meet. The way we have discussed today I think is a very hard issue for Iran. And then if you add in that there is mistrust that they have had a nuclear weapons development program in the past that the IAEA wants them to come clean on, then it may just be a bridge too far.

The CHAIRMAN. What is their ability with the time that has passed in the IAEA, the International Atomic Energy Administration—that reviews countries throughout the world—and their concerns or views that Iran was pursuing a nuclear weapons program. What is the ability of Iran to now undermine the facts as to what they had been doing as——

Dr. ALBRIGHT. Well, the IAEA has had, I do not know what it is, 10 meetings with Iran on this issue in the last several—2, 3 years—and their argument is pretty clear. The documentation is fabricated. People are lying. You know, there is no evidence that is worth talking about. If something is substantially proven, they will say it is nothing to do with nuclear weapons.

They tell the IAEA you cannot talk to the people you want to talk to. The IAEA has asked to go to several sites, not just the Parchin site. They are not allowed to go to those sites. And recently, in the last year or so, the IAEA was told you cannot ask about procurement information anymore, and yet that is a large part of the evidence on some aspects of the military dimension.

So, and in a meeting that just happened last week, I think the IAEA tried to say it was constructive, but they also issued a statement saying there was no progress. But we hope there will be progress in the next meeting, which is in late October.

The CHAIRMAN. Finally, what I call breakout capacity, you have a somewhat different definition of it, but it is the same. We are talking about the same thing. Just give the committee a sense of how you come to the calculus in which you have come to, the timeframe that you developed.

Dr. ALBRIGHT. Yes, the calculation is based on a set of work that we do with centrifuge specialists at University of Virginia, one of whom used to head what is called the physics program or the U.S. centrifuge program in the United States. It was the theoretical program for centrifuges.

And we look at the calculations. We then look at how many centrifuges Iran is installing and what rate that is projected over the next year or so. We then assumed that the time we are worried about is when they would have enough 20 percent enriched uranium that would allow for the fastest breakout, and then we assume that they could make the switchover from low-enriched uranium production to weapon-grade uranium production faster than they can today.

And then we came up with this estimate of mid-2014. And I must say the criticism we are hearing is that it is sooner, particularly if they can deploy large numbers of these advanced centrifuges. We still think it is mid-2014 is a solid date. I would be very interested to knowing how the administration thinks about this and its calculations.

Our specialists at UVA came out of the enrichment program of the United States and is aware of how the U.S. Government does its calculations, and we do not see major differences. One difference that I will point out is we look at minimum times. And we have heard this in previous hearings.

We look at minimum times. The U.S. Government tends to look at more likely times. And so, I know we can—because from a policy point of view or the implications of our work, we think the minimum time is the one to know, where the likely time, which certainly would be longer, has less policy relevance but still is an important number.

The CHAIRMAN. So mid-2014 is 8 months from now—8 or 9 months from now. And you say to the extent that there is criticism of your institute's work is that it might be on the shorter time, not the——

Dr. ALBRIGHT. Yes, that is right.

The CHAIRMAN. Senator Corker.

Senator CORKER. Thank you, Mr. Chairman.

And thank each of you for being here. It is obviously a great privilege for us to have three very knowledgeable folks in this area to help us as we think through this. So thank you for making yourselves available and being here today.

And I would ask Mr. Albright and Jeffrey, Mr. Takeyh sort of gave an internal assessment of sort of the politics inside Iran and where the files exist and all of those kind of things, and I would just like to ask first, do you all generally agree with his assessment of the internal situation in Iran itself?

Dr. ALBRIGHT. Yes, I cannot speak—I depend on Ray for these kinds of things. So I do not have independent judgment on the internal politics in Iran.

Senator CORKER. Yes?

Ambassador JEFFREY. Yes, and I think most experts also would agree with him.

Senator CORKER. And just I know, Mr. Albright, you talked a little bit about the things that we know. I guess, based on especially some of the things Mr. Takeyh said, and our general sense of the way Iran as a country is, I guess you would assume there are also a lot of activities that are occurring that we do not know about. Is that correct?

Dr. ALBRIGHT. I think that is well known. I mean, you can just look at what the inspectors can do. They cannot look at where centrifuges are made. They do not have any idea how many have been made.

They do not get a good picture of the research and development of advanced centrifuges. So there is many things that are not known. We do not know if they are building a third centrifuge plant, and that assessment is based on them saying they would and that the last public statement was we will start building one summer of 2013. And that statement has not been corrected or changed by the Iranians.

So there is a lot of things we do not know. Where there is hope with Iran is that they will be more transparent. I mean, in these discussions, Iranians have said they are willing to be more transparent and perhaps answer these kind of questions. Where there is problems is when they say that is pretty much all they are going to do in terms of really limiting and avoiding real limits on their nuclear program.

Senator CORKER. So we have, you know, really bright and knowledgeable people like you come in to share with us the way things are. And then, at the end of the day, I guess our role is to take some kind of action. I mean, that is what we do here. Should we do something in addition to what has occurred?

And sometimes I think, you know, we have to be the bad cop to push along the good cop, if you will, the people who are actually involved in the negotiations. And then, on the other hand, sometimes we can do things unbeknownst—not necessarily in this area, I think we have been very productive—but we can do things that actually hamper.

And so, I would ask you this, all three of you, based on the way you see things evolving, what is it that the United States Congress should do relative to what is happening right now to support, to enhance, or not do to try to get to the end that we all believe has a very small chance of being successful? But what would you advise us to be involved in right now, all three of you?

Dr. ALBRIGHT. Yes, I think, let me first, on the hamper, I think I would agree with Ambassador Sherman that it is better to delay passage of new sanctions laws until Iran is tested. I mean, she gave the date of October 15. So it is actually not much of a wait, although I would expect the meeting in mid-October could be complicated, and the message that testing may not be clear.

So I think there may be a need to hold off a little longer. Where I think the Congress is very helpful is that you do these sanctions laws. I think they have been critically important in creating the pressure on Iran and that if Iran continues to increase its nuclear program, which will be clear in November in the next IAEA report whether that is true or not, then I think increased nuclear work should be met with increased sanctions.

And the other thing is that the U.S. Government is clearly not trying to reveal its negotiating position, and I think that is good. But I think that it is important that there be mechanisms set up, and Congress, I think, can play an important role of what is a good negotiating position and what is not. And it can be done on a technical level, where it does not have to become that politicized of what are the steps that are needed in order to reach the point where the United States would have assurance that Iran is not going to build nuclear weapons?

And anyone can come up with 20 conditions, but how do you then take the subset of that and, in a sense, how do you optimize it and decide that it is enough? And I think there needs to be quite a bit of discussion about that involving, I would hope, the U.S. Government. But I think Ambassador Sherman made it pretty clear that they are not going to participate on an unclassified level, but I think the American public needs to know.

There is a lot of confusion about what is necessary to accomplish. And particularly if you add in war weariness, there may be a lot of pressure to accept a deal that is really not going to solve this problem.

Senator CORKER. Thank you.

Mr. Jeffrey.

Ambassador JEFFREY. I thought that the position that Secretary Sherman laid out is reasonable from the standpoint of someone who has been in the administration, this one and ones in the past. You always want the maximum flexibility.

On the other hand, you cannot let that dangle out forever. As we have heard, you have a mid-2014 time period. Other experts I know—Olli Heinonen, formerly of the IAEA, and others at the Washington Institute—would agree with these kind of timelines. So we do not have a lot of time.

It is very important that Iran understand that the charm offensive means nothing. What is important is what it does. If it does not take action, there will be more sanctions.

Now I cannot talk to exactly what the sanctions would be. That is something that you folks are working on up here and will be back and forth in the administration, as Wendy Sherman said, because there are some that are more effective than others. What we do know is the sanctions that you folks have put in place are extremely effective, both in harming the Iranian economy and in bringing the Iranians to at least consider some kind of deal.

In order to avoid sanctions which were put in place by the United Nations in 2010, they accepted a somewhat flawed deal from the Turks and the Brazilians just before. So they do respond to pressure. That is a good thing.

So my recommendation would be give the administration the flexibility to see where Iran is going. We will know pretty soon the basic outlines. It may take more time, just like the agreement between Secretary Kerry and Lavrov over a month ago on the Syrian chemical situation was in place, and then it took a good number of weeks before the final resolution could be hammered out. But it was going in the right direction.

If this goes in the right direction, you can hold off. If it is going in the wrong direction, you need to consider what further action would be appropriate.

Senator CORKER. Mr. Takeyh.

Dr. TAKEYH. So thank you.

I think, looking at the Islamic Republic for quite a long time as I have, unfortunately, I would say that Islamic Republic responds to pressure, and that has been sort of validated by their response to the sanctions measures that have been enacted.

So I guess the argument for pause in terms of passing of the legislation that is in front of you do not make all that much sense to me because I actually think that its expeditious passage could help the administration in their negotiations. While I am not quite sure if the pause, October 14 or whatever it is, past that date.

I certainly anticipate that given that how heightened expectations are, the parties are going to emerge from the mid-October meetings suggesting they had frank, good discussions, and they will proceed along those lines. I do not think, given how high the expectations have been, unfortunately, inflated, they can say otherwise.

The second thing that I would suggest is along the lines of a rather poignant series of questions that Senator Rubio asked. We kind of understand the parameters of a deal that the international community is seeking to negotiate with Iran. We understand the Iranian position that they require an indigenous enrichment capability, even though they do not have natural uranium depositories.

So they want domestic enrichment. The Russians, the Chinese, and the Europeans have largely conceded that. The position of the executive branch, as Senator Rubio demonstrated, was evolving.

The United States Congress, Senate or the House, should actually have their own say, as a collective body, not as individual Senators, about whether they think a final status agreement would entail domestic enrichment on Iranian soil and, if so, under which modalities and so on.

Everybody has expressed their point of view about this issue as a collective body except the United States legislative branch. Individual Senators have a position. At times, those positions are congregated in a letter and so on, but maybe you want to consider some sort of a resolution to that effect.

And if the position—if the United States Congress wants to join the prevailing consensus that the Islamic Republic should have enrichment rights, then that is fine. But you should express a collective position.

Senator CORKER. Thank you all very much. Thank you.

The CHAIRMAN. Thank you.

Senator Rubio.

Senator RUBIO. I will just take it from there and tell you why I feel so strongly about that. I think in any negotiation the first thing we have to understand is who are you dealing with? Because that tells you a lot about the parameters of a negotiation and where it can head.

So here is who I think we are dealing with. First, I think we are dealing with a country run by a bunch of liars because this is a country that has gone around saying—that their program is peaceful and that they will never develop nuclear weapons. And yet there are reams of open source reporting about the fact that at multiple times in the past, they have had an aggressive nuclear program. And I do not think anyone in the world now looks at what they are doing and concludes that they are not trying to build the capacity for weaponized nuclear capability.

Here is another piece of evidence as to the belief that they are liars. They say that they do not have any intent to develop nuclear weapons, but they are investing a lot of time and energy on long-range missiles. Now what do you put on a long-range missile? You put a weapon. You put a nuclear weapon. It is the only reason to have one.

So they are developing all of these ICBMs for one of two reasons. They are either planning one heck of a fireworks show, or they intend to put a nuclear warhead on a rocket and to be able to threaten the world with it.

And the third reason why they are liars is because they admit to it. This is interesting. This is from Prime Minister Netanyahu's speech at the United Nations, and I am going to quote from it.

He talks about a 2011 book where Rouhani basically writes, and he quotes, "While we were talking to the Europeans in Tehran, we were installing equipment in Isfahan." Now for those who do not know, the Isfahan facility is an indispensable part of Iran's nuclear weapons program. That is where uranium ore, called yellow cake, is converted into an enrichable form.

Rouhani boasted, and he quotes, "By creating a calm environment, we were able to complete the work in Isfahan." Basically, he fooled the world once and now thinks he can fool it again.

So, number one, we are dealing with a bunch of liars. The second thing we are dealing with is a bunch of really evil people. I know that is a term that gets thrown around loosely, but here is the evidence.

They actively participate in the slaughter of innocent people in Syria and in other parts of the world. They actively destabilize their neighbors in Bahrain, in Lebanon, now in Iraq, and in other places. They provide support to Hezbollah so they can fire rockets into civilian areas of Israel.

Two years ago, they tried to assassinate the Ambassador of Saudi Arabia in this very city, okay? This is who we are negotiating with. We are not negotiating with Belgium. We are not negotiating with Luxembourg. We are negotiating with a government, a country run by evil liars.

And when you negotiate with evil liars, everything that you—all of your lines have to be clearly marked out, and the verifications have to be stronger. I mean, we are dealing with some very dangerous people here. And so, that is why I feel so passionately about being very clear about what our position is.

And I believe that our—and you can—I am open to the comments of the folks who are here today because certainly you spend a lot of time on this. But I, for the life of me, do not understand why the official policy of the United States is not as follows.

Number one, you stop enrichment of uranium. Number two, you allow the existing stockpiles to be transferred and removed from your country. Number three, take down all of those facilities you have that only serve the purpose of enriching to weapons grade, places like the underground secret facilities that they have in Qom or the centrifuges in Natanz. And number four, stop working on these heavy water reactors that are going to be used to produce plutonium.

This should be our offer. Our offer should be you do these four things, and then maybe the sanctions start to get lessened. But this notion that somewhere in between that there is the capability of leaving in place the infrastructure and the enrichment capabilities so that 5 years from now, 8 years from now, when they have now fully developed their ICBMs. They have now fully developed the ability to turn that into a warhead, 5 or 6 years from now they can decide, you know what, we are going to get a weapon because fill in the blank. They can make up any excuse they want.

This is who we are dealing with here, and there is precedent for this. This is what North Korea did. This is what Pakistan did, and this is what they are going to do. These guys are going to get a weapon because they view it as security for the regime. They view it as a way to become the dominant power in the region.

And by the way, we should be scared of it not just because of Iran. A nuclear Iran means we will see a nuclear Saudi Arabia. We will see potentially a nuclear Turkey, and even potentially one day, a nuclear Egypt.

And so, I just do not understand all the silliness about we are dealing with these guys. We are going to sit down. We are going to—they are buying for time. That is all they are doing. They are trying to—this is the bottom-line mandate that they have.

What can we do to lessen these sanctions in the short term while continuing the slow, steady progression? Maybe we will slow down the progression, but they will get there nonetheless.

Because ultimately if they reach a point where they can break out, they do not have to break out. Just the ability to break out gives them a tremendous amount of leverage on the world while they continue to develop their ICBMs for this fireworks show that they are apparently planning or for the ability to threaten the east coast of the United States.

So I just hope that as policymakers, we start to take this—well, I know that the committee does—take this very seriously for what it is. Stop playing games. This is a very serious issue, and we are dealing with very dangerous people who while they say all these nice things out there, their actions are clear.

They are assassinating, destabilizing, you know, all the things that they are doing. These are evil liars that we are dealing with.

The CHAIRMAN. All right. I think you should be more passionate about how you feel on this issue. [Laughter.]

But it is a very serious issue, and I appreciate your statements.

Let me just do one final thing because my colleague Senator Corker, in his very thoughtful way as always, has asked what should the Congress do or not do? And several of you responded that the Congress should not necessarily proceed with any additional sanctions at this time until we see what happens on the 15th and 16th.

And let me ask you this question. So the 15th and 16th comes. We have what will diplomatically be referred to as we have some substantive discussions. We believe that it is worthy of continuing forward, and these negotiations never turn into a few days after that. They turn into weeks after that, if not months.

And so, the time clicks by. In the interim, nothing stops in the process itself as it exists today. And so, what is so wrong, when Dr.

Albright says that mid-2014—so giving the whole month of October, November, December, and then through June, that is 9 months. And to the extent that he says the institute has received criticism is that it may be shorter, not longer.

So 9 months, what is wrong with the Congress of the United States pursuing a perfecting sanctions regime that would seek greater reductions in petroleum that would look at some critical issues that the Iranians are still using even with the regimes that exist now, such as the use of steel in their automotive sector and shipping sector and what not.

And which never get enforced until way beyond those 9 months but gives the administration, as they are sitting there, the reality to look what is coming around the corner from the Congress if we cannot have now some real significant movement by Iran.

None of the sanctions—and I have been the author of all of them, along with Senator Kirk and others—none of the sanctions have ever gone into effect immediately. They have a timeframe for implementation. They give an opportunity for countries to join us in the effort and to prepare, for example, in the reductions of petroleum.

So it seems to me that—and some of us are contemplating in this new round of sanctions for the first time saying, but if the Iranians meet the responsibilities that have been laid out by the Security Council, then these new round of sanctions can cease, which gives a message to them that they are concerned. I often hear they are concerned that even if they struck an agreement that they ultimately are not sure that the Congress would remove the sanctions that exist.

So if we created both a carrot and a stick whose implementation would not take place beyond the timeframe of the breakout period if nothing goes unabated, how is that not a positive for the administration versus it being a negative?

Dr. TAKEYH. I think the argument for pause makes sense if there is corresponding pause. Namely, if the Iranians also pause their activities. They are required by six U.N. Security Council resolutions, perhaps seven, to suspend their nuclear activities. They have not done so. They continue—if they pause spending $500 million a month in Syria to prop up the Assad dynasty.

But there is no corresponding pause on their side. Their activities continue to go on on the nuclear front, on the proliferation front, on the terrorism front, and so on. So the argument of pause does not make much sense to me.

I would make pitch for one additional idea that you may want to consider, which I have done so elsewhere. Namely, establishing an Iran human rights commission similar to the Helsinki Commission that was established or the China Commission, which essentially focuses on Iran's human rights abuses and can prescribe measures to deal with that.

It is a conversation that can bring Democrats and Republicans together, and then also the executive branch would have observation status in that. And that would essentially focus the issue.

Iran today is not just a proliferator, is not just a sponsor of terrorism. It leads the globe in execution of minors. It is second in executions per capita to China. There is grotesque and important human rights abuses that I think requires greater degree of accentuation and perhaps some similar legislative remedy as well.

The CHAIRMAN. Ambassador Jeffrey.

Ambassador JEFFREY. It is hard ever to argue against more sanctions on a perpetual aggressor and war criminal state like Iran. As I said earlier, this is a long-term conflict. But rather than say yes or no to even general sanctions, I would just give you one perspective.

To my left, I have a guy who knows Iran far better than I. To my right, I have someone who knows the nuclear account far better than I. So what can I contribute to this thing?

What I would suggest is, first, I know a little bit about dealing with foreign governments because I have spent about 40 years doing it, and last, I know a lot about wars and military engagements because I have been involved in a lot of them. So what I would say is in figuring out your position, remember that there are many other actors besides the United States and Iran in this thing.

We rely on other countries to accommodate us by carrying out these sanctions. They are the ones who cut imports of oil, not we. We put penalties on them if they do, but they have to decide that going along with us and avoiding the penalties is more important than bringing in the oil and such.

And under certain circumstances, depending on what the sanctions are, they may or may not at some point go along with us. So that is the devil in the details. We do need this international coalition not only for the sanctions, but also—and it is not at the back, but at the front of my mind with everything we do with Iran on this issue—if we have to go to military force.

Because I think that is an extremely important threat, and I think it is our last possibility. And I have spent 4 years in Iraq and Vietnam. I know what it is like sending our troops into combat when they do not have the support of the international community, and it is very important that whatever the administration does and whatever the Congress does, we ensure that we are not so out of synch with the rest of the international community that we are isolated because that is going to be a bad place to be if this gets really serious.

The CHAIRMAN. I appreciate that, and the fact is, is that in our—sometimes in the sanction regime effort, you have to lead and you get others to follow or to join. I should not say ''follow,'' but to join. And that has actually been our experience here.

And then at some points, others led, and we followed. The European Union was on its way to a total oil embargo before we moved in a certain direction—or asked for further reduction. So there has been to some degree in this respect a concert of efforts.

And I agree with you we need to maintain that, but it just seems to me that the simple threat of a new round without that taking its bite well within a certain period of time beyond the breakout period is—I do not understand what the cause for alarm is.

Dr. Albright, we will give you the final word.

Dr. ALBRIGHT. Yes, I do not think it is cause for alarm, but I think they have to be justified carefully. Because it is going to be asking allies to do things and even adversaries, if I can characterize China that way. So I think it has to be demonstrated that they are needed and justified.

The CHAIRMAN. Well, I agree with that, and we can definitely do that because we can show where Iran, even under the present sanctions regimes, has efforts to circumvent.

But I would simply say the world watches the slaughter in Syria and did not seem to want to act. And so, if we want to avoid the use of military force, which I believe needs to be a credible threat on the table as part of the equation, our best way to achieve that with the international community is to have Iran feel the domestic internal pressure that has, as you suggested, Mr. Takeyh, the Ayatollah and his dual portfolio come to a decision that the one not only has to be abated but maybe given up.

Dr. ALBRIGHT. Yes, I would add, though, that it should be motivated by what happens in October. I mean, and if they increase their program.

The CHAIRMAN. And if October comes and we hear that we have had some positive, substantive negotiations, but nothing has ceased. Let us say if October came and they said we are going to stop right now all enrichment. So let us stop another round of new sanctions.

I do not know. Maybe that might be something.

Dr. ALBRIGHT. Yes.

The CHAIRMAN. And then work from there. But if October comes and all we hear, which is what every P5+1 process has largely led to, is that we have had discussions and, you know, there has been some good environment, but nothing substantive has come. How many times of the October 15s do we have?

Dr. ALBRIGHT. I would argue—I guess I would take Ambassador Sherman at her word. I mean, this is the test, and if they do not pass it in October, then more action would occur, particularly in Congress.

The CHAIRMAN. Senator Corker.

Senator CORKER. Thank you.

I like that line of questioning very much, and I want to follow on to that. And again, thank you as witnesses for being here.

Mr. Takeyh, speaking of October, and we will know soon, obviously, but what is it that you think Iran's Foreign Minister is going to say to Secretary Kerry and Secretary Sherman?

Dr. TAKEYH. Well, my guess is they are going to try to suggest a greater degree of cooperation with the IAEA, which follows up on the promise of transparency. I think they have been for a long time interested in selling 20 percent enrichment, and to some extent, Prime Minister Netanyahu was remiss in emphasizing 20 percent when the problem has always been enrichment at 3.5 percent, and that is taking place at industrial scale in their towns.

The Iranians have been trying to sell the 20 percent for a long time. So I suspect they might table something about 20 percent in exchange for sanctions relief such as that may not directly involve the United States Congress, such as SWIFT accounts and so on and so forth. There are some aspects of the European commerce.

And I think so you kind of come out of that meeting by suggesting some agreements have been made that deal at least with the outer parameters of the nuclear issue. That would be, my guess would be on the upscale of what they could offer.

Senator CORKER. So back to what Senator Menendez was asking a minute ago or talking about the coalition. I guess one of the important elements, and I know that you all are, two of you are taking a slightly more cautious approach to sanctions. Takeyh may be a little bit more aggressive.

But an important part of what we are doing is keeping our coalition together. In other words, without the international coalition we have, the sanctions that we put in place generally do not have the impact that they otherwise would have. And I would just ask each of you to, from your perspective, tell us where you think that coalition is today relative to what is going on.

And just add to that, in the event, for instance, these talks are not successful, and I think most people here are pretty skeptical about where this is going to go. Let us say there isn't something that comes out tangibly very soon. How is the coalition hanging together well, and can it go on for a long period of time as it is today?

Dr. ALBRIGHT. Yes, I would say my experience would be that it is under stress. I mean, Europeans are being asked to do more and more, and there is some pushback now that was not there a year ago. So I think it is under stress, and that is why I think any new congressional sanctions should be motivated by what Iran does or does not do.

And I do share your concerns about mid-October because I just thought of this. In listening carefully to Ambassador Sherman, it appears that what could happen is Iran is being asked to respond to the Almaty proposal that was made, not to come up with a comprehensive framework agreement.

And so, you could end up in a situation where Iran responds to that proposal, which is very limited, and the proposal is public now. So we all know what is in it, and even if Iran said yes to that, it does not get anywhere near what is necessary.

So I think the administration needs to be pushed much more firmly about, is Iran going to provide in a sense a bottom line in October? And again, this would have to be nonpublic discussions, obviously, but I think we do need to know what exactly is going to happen in October, and is it the test that we think it will be?

And I think the world is going to be watching very carefully, and I think what happened in Syria is something to pay attention to, that military strikes are not that easy to get support for right now. And I think the sanctions could be the most important pressure that is brought to bear to get Iran to take the steps necessary to solve this.

And so, I would argue that after October that it really may be necessary to apply those sanctions or pass those sanctions in order to then get a deal.

Senator CORKER. Mr. Jeffrey.

Ambassador JEFFREY. First of all, David is right about the Almaty deal and the going-in position. I think there may be some hope for offline, direct United States-Iranian talks, which the door does seem to be open to. And the President also in his statement the other day did refer to the sort of sanctions relief that the

Iranians, I think, want. They would have to do very significant, verifiable, transparent, and meaning steps.

So I think that he, at least, is thinking about going beyond the Almaty proposals and try to find out what their bottom line is. They, of course, will also want to know what the international community's bottom line is in terms of sanctions. So that will be the play.

But in terms of your question specifically of the coalition, I am a little bit worried because I think the coalition, more than the United States, is being wooed a bit by Rouhani's performance at the United Nations, his various writings, and the rest of this stuff, and they are hoping that this era of good feelings will move forward. So we have to really educate them a bit that it is actions and not words, and the President has done a good job in this, and the more support he can get from Congress, the better on that.

In terms of China and purchasing oil, that is something that I think you have to look at the intelligence on, on what their options are and where they are. In terms of Russia, they have been very unhelpful on the Syrian thing in some respects, and I think they will exact a high price for further cooperation with us.

So there is some maneuvering back and forth. But I think that we are at a point where within the next few weeks, we can see whether the signs are going in that direction. Then the administration will have to convince allies, have to convince you, have to convince the American public, that it is worth either pursuing a negotiated track or return to the sanctions with the military option if the Iranians start crossing our redlines.

Dr. TAKEYH. I think on the strength of the coalition, the coalition has to be viewed as a large collection of countries with varying degrees of compliance records. The Russians and the Chinese have always been skeptical of sanctions, and they have tried to use their participation in these international meetings to negotiate their commerce and protect their commerce, particularly in terms of the Chinese and purchasing of Iranian oil.

I do not see a clamor in Europe for sanctions relief. I think the European Union has, in some ways, moved even beyond and ahead of the United States on these issues. So I do not see this notion of the European Union seeking to resume its relations, commercial relations with Iran. Even in absence of the sanctions, I think that would be difficult, given the high risk of Iranian commerce.

There are some Asian countries that continue to purchase Iranian oil, and here I think the Japanese or South Koreans have proven the most wobbly members of the sanctions committee, particularly in terms of the Japanese, which have even established their own insurance mechanism for transportation of the Iranian oil.

So the Asian trade I think continues, but I think the European trade at this point has been severed, and I am not quite sure if the Europeans are clamoring to come into it. And the categories of concerns that Europeans have tend to increase beyond those of the United States. They are much more focused on human rights issues, for instance, as more so than we have been. We have more of a proliferation-centric policy.

So I am not quite sure if the last couple of weeks in New York have changed the fundamentals of the coalition. Those who were weak continue to be weak. Those who were wobbly continue to be wobbly. And those who are resolute continue to be resolute.

Senator CORKER. Mr. Chairman, if I could, one last question? And you know, the chairman and I talked a great deal during the Syrian issue, you know, how we responded to that was very much going to impact the negotiations that we are talking about right now and Iran's response to us. And without giving any editorial comments, just wondering if you could share with us sort of the environment that we are in as far as the neighborhood as they watched the United States response in total.

There were a lot of episodes, and you know, how the neighborhood has responded to our response to Syria, but especially Iran. If you could just share with me what kind of environment it has created within those countries?

Ambassador JEFFREY. I would separate out the two. I think that the United States has a pretty convincing record of taking a tough position on Iran. I think that people generally believe that we are very serious about it. There are the sanctions that you have worked so hard on, and there are a lot of tough statements, most recently from the President a couple of days ago. But I think that people also look at what we have been doing.

The withdrawal from Iraq, which I was involved in; the impending withdrawal of all or most of our forces from Afghanistan; the talk of a pivot to Asia, even though I suspect 90 percent of the work of the foreign policy community still is in the Middle East; the way we not only led from behind on Libya—that may have been a pretty good idea—but the way we talked about and sort of praised ourselves for leading from behind; and most recently, the Syrian example has made, have all made our friends in the region question whether we are willing to use military force if things come to that.

And that is a very dangerous situation. That is how we got into the Korean war. We had not put South Korea inside our defense perimeter. We explicitly excluded it by Dean Acheson. The North Koreans invaded, with Russian encouragement, and we then engaged.

We do not want to stumble into a wall like that. We have to be very, very clear that we will use military force. Under the circumstances post Syria, this requires Presidential commitments and Presidential action and supporting action from the Congress to restore the belief, that is fundamental to everything that I have experienced in the last 40 years all around the world, that the United States and its friends and allies, as part of an international coalition, will act to preserve threats to the international order.

That is being questioned now, sir.

Dr. ALBRIGHT. One thing I would like to add to that is—well, two things. One is certainly the Gulf States are very concerned— I mean, they have made that pretty apparent—in what the United States is going to do.

Now question I would have is, is based on if we think about deterring Iran from breaking out. I mean, even now we think they could do it relatively quickly. I mean, a month, month and a half.

I mean, the inspection can detect that and give timely warning that it is taking place. But that does not leave a lot of time for a military response.

As breakout times shrink, it is pretty clear that the military—whichever one is going to do it, whether it is Israel or the United States—is going to have to be striking within a few days. And has the Syrian situation confused whether the President has the authority to do that.

And again, this is not a case where there is clear evidence of someone violating a major international agreement, namely the Nonproliferation Treaty. So it is not a preemptive strike. It is an action has been taken that is judged as trying to build nuclear weapons. Can the United States—does the Obama administration feel it has the authority to act within a few days with a military response?

The CHAIRMAN. Mr. Takeyh, you are going to have the last word of this hearing.

Dr. TAKEYH. Sure, in terms of regional situation, the Middle East is a region that continuously divides against itself, and it has divided against itself today. There is an interregional cold war on the one hand led by Saudi Arabia, on the other hand by Iran. And this is a cold war that is playing itself out in the gulf, in Bahrain, even though I think the Saudis' claims are overstated. It is playing itself out in Iraq, playing itself out in Lebanon, and certainly playing itself out in Syria.

So that is the sort of a division we see in the region. It is a cold war that is likely to be more protracted because it is predicated on sectarian identities, Shia versus Sunnis and that sort of a thing. So the Middle East is in a particularly unstable and dangerous period.

The United States, obviously, has a role in terms of reassuring its allies and deterring its adversaries. It is a role that it chooses to play however maladroitly or successfully it may want to.

The CHAIRMAN. Well, thank you all. It has been a very interesting and helpful panel. I appreciate it.

With the thanks of the committee, the hearing's record will remain open until the close of business tomorrow for members' questions.

And with that, this hearing is adjourned.

[Whereupon, at 12:47 p.m., the hearing was adjourned.]

---

ADDITIONAL MATERIAL SUBMITTED FOR THE RECORD

RESPONSES OF UNDER SECRETARY WENDY SHERMAN TO QUESTIONS
SUBMITTED BY SENATOR ROBERT CORKER

*Question.* Is the administration considering including Iran in upcoming negotiations to achieve a political settlement to the conflict in Syria? If so, why? What constructive role do you feel Iran can play in those negotiations? How will their participation affect the Syrian opposition?

Answer. We believe that whoever attends the Geneva Conference on Syria must accept and publicly support the Geneva Communique, including the key point of establishing by mutual consent a new transition governing body with full executive authorities. We have been clear that Iran has played a destructive role in this crisis by sending Quds Forces into Syria, by helping Hezbollah fight in Syria, and by organizing the dispatch of Iraqi Shia militiamen to fight in Syria, all directly contributing to the Assad regime's brutality against the Syrian people. If Iran were to endorse and embrace full implementation of the Geneva Communique publicly, we would view the possibility of their participation more openly. So far it has not done so.

*Question.* We have established that Iran is already dangerously close to achieving critical breakout capability. If we give you 3 months to test diplomacy they will be closer. What is our strategy to move Iran back from breakout in the event diplomacy fails?

*Answer.* We believe there is a window for diplomacy, but time is not unlimited, and the President has consistently said that all options are on the table. We are confident that the international community would have sufficient time to respond to any Iranian breakout effort. We continue to closely monitor Iran's nuclear program for any signs that the regime has made an explicit decision to develop a nuclear weapon or is operating secret facilities for covert production of enriched uranium.

*Question.* President Obama has repeatedly emphasized the fact, both at the United Nations and in his statement after the phone call with Rouhani, that Ayatollah Khamenei has issued a fatwa against nuclear weapons. Are you using the fatwa as a serious factor in assessing Iranian intentions?

*Answer.* On September 26 in New York, at a speech at the Council on Foreign Relations, President Rouhani paraphrased Ayatollah Khamenei and stated, ''The development, production, stockpiling and use of nuclear weapons are contrary to the Islamic norms.'' As President Obama has stated many times, we remain committed to ensuring Iran does not obtain a nuclear weapon—and as a result, we were heartened to learn about the fatwa against nuclear weapons.

But the fatwa itself is not the basis for assessing Iranian intentions. Iran must match its rhetoric with meaningful, transparent, and verifiable actions. This has always been our stance.

*Question.* What is your current assessment of the amount Iran has in its foreign exchange reserves? Under current conditions, when will Iran run out of money?

*Answer.* Independent experts estimate that Iran's foreign currency reserves were valued around 70–80 billion USD in 2012. In theory, if Iran used only its foreign currency reserves instead of earnings derived from trade surpluses with other countries, the Iranian Government would have about 8 months before running out of money to pay for imports. However, because most of Iran's foreign reserves are extremely difficult to access, the period is less than 3 months under this scenario.

Most of Iran's reserves are partially or completely inaccessible largely due to the administration implementing key provisions of the Iran Threat Reduction and Syria Human Rights Act of 2012 (TRA) on February 6, 2013. In addition to putting restrictions on Iran's foreign currency reserve holdings, provisions in the TRA restrict Iran's ability to use oil revenue held in foreign financial institutions. Due to the success of the TRA, the Iranian Government can only use the vast majority of its overseas holdings to facilitate bilateral trade with countries that import Iranian oil, or to facilitate humanitarian trade.